A PRAYER PRIMER

A
Prayer
Primer

A Guide on How to Pray in Public
Erwin J. Kolb

Publishing House
St. Louis

Erwin J. Kolb

Concordia Publishing House, St. Louis, Missouri
Copyright © 1982 by Concordia Publishing House
Manufactured in the United States of America

Library of Congress Cataloging in Publication Data
Kolb, Erwin J.
    A prayer primer.

    1. Prayer. I. Title.
BV226.K64   264'.1   81-14358
ISBN 0-570-03843-X   AACR2

1 2 3 4 5 6 7 8 9 10   MAL   91 90 89 88 87 86 85 84 83 82

Dedication

To the elders of the churches I served as pastor who patiently struggled with me to learn how to pray.

And

To the students of Concordia Teachers College, Seward, who studied and prayed together in our Bible Study—Prayer Group, STP (Study, Testimony, Prayer).

Contents

Introduction

I was an eager young pastor. The elders of the congregation were excited about their new pastor and envisioned great things for the congregation as a result of my coming. At one of our first elders' meetings, I proposed that we schedule one elder to be on duty for each of the Sunday services. His duties would be to coordinate all of the details of the service with the pastor, and then just before the service pray with the pastor for the guidance and blessing of God on that particular service. I continued to explain my vision. The name of the elder assigned to each service would be published in the Sunday bulletin so that the members would know who was on duty that day, possibly express any concerns, and, finally, know who was praying with the pastor for the service.

The only problem was that none of the elders had ever prayed out loud in public! I could see it on their faces. They were ready to abandon the idea or resign as elders. I hurriedly explained that we would first teach them how to construct prayers and practice praying in our elders' meetings, and then if they still wanted to, they could write out their prayers and read them. Reluctantly they agreed. Today, 30 years later, that congregation maintains the same practice: the elders lead in prayer—out loud—in the sacristry before each service. Recently one of those first elders said, "I'm still grateful for that experience. Learning how to pray in public stimulated new growth in my spiritual life."

But not only elders need to learn how to pray in public. Envision yourself in a situation like this:

You are in a home Bible study with 10 other people from the church. You came because the Women's Missionary League had a special program and your friend invited you. At the close of a lively discussion the leader says, "Now let's close with a circle prayer. Each one in turn pray about what's on your heart tonight." What would you do? You have never prayed out loud in a group before? Can you do it?

Or suppose you are visiting a friend who is seriously ill.

You find it difficult to know what to say as you leave but you manage the words, "I'll pray for you." Your friend takes your hand and says, "Thank you so much, but will you also pray for me right now?" Would you be able to fill this request?

You can learn how to pray out loud in public! That has been demonstrated not only by elders, by Women Missionary League members, but also by many other Christians. This book is designed to help you learn how to do it. And if you practice what this book suggests, with God's help, you will be able to do it.

Perhaps you have read other books on prayer. There are many on the market, and their number is multiplying. But most of the books in the past have dealt with such things as the theology of prayer, the development of a personal prayer life in your private devotional relationship with the Lord, or the explanation of the Lord's Prayer. But this book is different. It has one goal which governs its contents, namely, to teach its reader how to pray out loud in public. It will deal with subjects like the theology of prayer or the Lord's Prayer only to the extent that they contribute to the achievement of that goal.

We have given this book the title *A Prayer Primer*. Some of the reviewers of the first draft manuscript read the word in the title as "Primer," which means according to the dictionary definition, "a small book of elementary principles," such as an elementary book for teaching children to read. Other reviewers understood that word as "prime-r," which is spelled the same way as "primer" but means "that which primes." This book can be thought of as both. It is a book of elementary principles about prayer. But it is also a book which hopes to "prime" the reader so that the composition of personal prayers and praying out loud in public will be achieved.

Our approach in this book challenges one of the assumptions often made in books on prayer, which is that if one learns to pray in his private devotions, he will be able to pray in public. This is only partly true. It depends on what kinds of prayers are being spoken in that private devotional life. It can be, as is often the case, merely reciting memorized words or reading printed prayers, and that is of little help in *ex corde* praying in public. (*Ex corde* refers to "out of the heart" prayers spoken in one's own words and not the words of others, printed or memorized.)

But if one's private devotional life is such that it includes talking to God about personal needs and concerns in personal, out-of-the-heart words, then this kind of prayer life enables praying out loud in public. In this case, the statement is true that one's "private prayer life determines the quality of his public praying." Then it is like an iceberg where eight-ninths is hidden under the water and only one-ninth is visible to the human eye. So the eight-ninths of one's prayer life is one's private prayer to God, which no one usually sees, and the one-ninth, the visible part, is the praying out loud in public. But they are both of the same substance.

In discussing prayer in public one sometimes hears it said that Christians are not supposed to pray in public or in groups, but only in the privacy of their own rooms. That idea is drawn from the words of Jesus in Matthew 6:6, "When you pray, go into your room and shut the door and pray to your Father who is in secret; And your Father who sees in secret will reward you." Jesus is here condemning prayer for show, as was done by the Pharisees praying on the street corner to be seen by others. The Scripture is full of examples and encouragement to God's people to pray together in groups, as will be discussed throughout this book. (See especially the section on "Praying with Others" in Chapter 4.)

"Praying in public" does not necessarily mean praying in front of a large group of people. It might mean praying with only one other person, with your own family, or in a small group. Remember the promise of Jesus: "If two agree on earth about anything they ask, it will be done for them by My Father in heaven. For where two or three are gathered in My name, there am I in the midst of them" (Matthew 18:19-20).

11

The method that we are using in this book is to organize our discussion of praying in public around four words which are an acrostic on the word "pray."

P is for Praise
R is for Remember
A is for Ask
Y is for Yield

After an introductory chapter on "Getting Ready to Pray," we discuss each of the four words in the acrostic on PRAY in four separate chapters. Each chapter will conclude with a section on "Bible Study and Action," which is intended for further study in the Scriptures on the subject of that chapter. It also offers some suggestions to put that material into practice. The Bible Study and Action section can be used for private study, for discussion by a group in a Bible class, or in a group of Christians who meet together to help each other learn how to pray, such as a board of elders, a church council, a women's group, a youth group, or a home study group. As you now begin to move into the content of this book, one final thought about the attitude with which you read. An illustration will emphasize the point. A speaker said in his address, "I believe in a cold shower the first thing when one gets up in the morning." After he concluded his presentation, a curious listener asked, "How does a cold shower feel the first thing when you get out of bed?"

"I don't know," the speaker responded. "I said that I believed in it, not that I did it."

You, the reader, can believe in the benefits of prayer but not learn how to pray. You can say that you want to learn how to pray in public and not learn. You only learn how to pray by praying. The attitude that we encourage is one of openness to the content of this book and willingness to practice the suggestions that it makes about praying. Then, God willing, you will learn how to pray in public.

All the Scripture passages quoted are in the Revised Standard Version, unless otherwise indicated.

Chapter 1
Get Ready to Pray

A holy man of India was bothered in his meditations by mice that played in the quiet secluded place where he went to pray. They distracted his focus on the divine. To remedy the situation, the holy man bought a cat and tied it near him during his meditations. That alleviated the irritation.

Some of the disciples of the holy man noticed that whenever he meditated, he had his cat tied near him. They assumed that the presence of a cat was an essential ingredient of meditation, so they imitated him. In this way the idea developed that one needed a cat in order to meditate and be in communion with the divine.[1]

The church, through the centuries, has developed many customs in connection with prayer. These customs may be no more meaningful than the presence of a cat in meditation, and their real origins may be just as obscure. In learning how to pray in public, we must first unlearn some of the customs that hinder prayer. We must bypass previous traditions and learn new ways of thinking about prayer. This chapter suggests some ways of thinking about prayer that are intended to prepare us both mentally and spiritually for learning how to pray in public.

1. Overcome Previous Habits

What would be your first reaction if the pastor or the chairman of your committee at church called you and asked, "Will you open the meeting with prayer tonight?" Find a prayer book? Why is this often the first response? Perhaps because that is what we have done in the past. We have read prayers from prayer books, seen other people read their prayers, and even watched the pastor read printed prayers. In fact, many pastors, as well as their people, get so steeped in liturgies and litanies, that they find it difficult to make their own prayers or to pray *ex corde* (from the heart, without a printed page). If you are going to learn to pray in public, however, that is the kind of response that you must change.

Perhaps, however, you are brave enough to try to write a prayer of your own. But to get some help you go to a book on prayer, or dig out some notes of a class you once had which described the various elements which go into making a proper prayer. You then try to compose a prayer which contains all of those elements. The elements might be:

> A greeting or address
> Thanksgiving or adoration
> Confession
> Petition
> Intercession
> Dedication
> Close

As you work your way through these parts of a prayer, you will find it very awkward to include all of these elements in a prayer to begin a meeting of the ushers' staff or the Sunday school teachers. That is not surprising—most people do. Those ingredients may fit some prayers for some occasions—but usually they don't all fit into the same prayer!

Variations of the above outline are used today in many books on prayer. One of the outlines a little easier to use describes prayer in terms of the four letters in the word ACTS: Adoration, Confession, Thanksgiving, and Supplication. This is simpler than a six- or seven-word outline, but again for the time being bypass this approach. All of these ingredients in a prayer outline may be used to analyze prayers and to enrich prayer life, but for a person who is just learning how to compose his own public prayers these can be obstacles that make learning how to pray in public so difficult that one is driven back to reading the prayers that others have written. Come back to the outlines later if you like, but, for now, lay them aside and think of prayer in a much more simple way, as just talking to God.

2. Think of Praying as Talking to God

Some of the popular definitions of prayer which help us to think about prayer as "talking to God" are:

"A heart-to-heart talk with God"

"Heaven's telephone that is never out of order"

"A conversation between two persons who love each other"

If you think about praying as talking to God, you don't have to worry about whether you are using a proper outline or saying things in the right order or with the right words. Maxie Dunnam confesses in her workbook on prayer: "One of the great difficulties of my life was to believe that I could actually talk with God, that he would hear and listen and respond to me."[2]

If prayer is just talking to God, then is it true that those people who are "good talkers" can also be "good pray-ers." That is partly true! People who are used to working with words and know how to put them together in conversation will find it easier to express themselves when talking to God in public. But that only means that their prayers flow easier and may be longer. It does not mean that those who talk less and find it hard to think of things to say in conversation cannot learn how to pray in public. Their public prayers may be shorter, may be spoken more deliberately and with simpler words, but they can learn to pray in public, speaking in the style and manner that is natural to them.

But praying is a special kind of talking to God, it is talking which expresses your relationship with God.

3. Be Aware of Your Relationship to God

Lois Johnson in the book *Either Way I Win* described how her own prayer life grew while she struggled with cancer, and she says to the reader, "You'll discover that prayer is the language of relationship."[3] We can talk more easily to a person that we have come to know and respect and love than we can with the stranger who is distant or of whom we are uncertain.

When one of the disciples of Jesus asked Him, "Lord,

teach us to pray," He said, "When you pray, pray like this, 'Our Father who art in heaven' " (Luke 11:1-2). Although God was their Creator and Lord, the Almighty Ruler of heaven and earth, they could talk to Him because He was also their Father and they were His children. So Luther points out: "God would by these words tenderly invite us to believe that we are His true children, so that we may with all boldness and confidence ask Him as dear children ask their dear father."

Prayer is truly a privilege. It is the privilege of those who have become children of God by faith in Christ Jesus. Unless we are in that relationship, we cannot approach the presence of the Almighty nor talk to Him in a personal way.

Hallesby in his book *Prayer,* which has become something of a classic on that subject, elaborates on the meaning of prayer flowing out of a relationship similar to that of a child to its father. He speaks of prayer as a special attitude of the mind and heart. The attitude of a child is first of all helplessness or dependence, as a small child is dependent upon its parents. A child in the second place has faith. He is confident that his father has the power to help and will help because he cares about him. These attitudes, helplessness and faith, are immediately recognized by God as prayer, whether they take the form of words or not. It is a cry from "your heart to the heart of God. . . . He hears it from the very moment that you are seized with helplessness and He becomes engaged at once in hearing and answering the prayer of your helplessness."[4] Hallesby summarizes, "Without faith our helplessness would be only a vain cry of distress in the night. . . . Helplessness united with faith produces prayer."[5]

The helplessness that leads to prayer might be compared to the boy who was trying to move a heavy stone in the yard when his father arrived home. The father watched his son struggle for a few minutes and then asked him, "Are you using all of your resources?"

Surprised, the boy answered, "Sure, I am, can't you see how hard I am trying?

"But," the father replied, "you haven't asked me to help."

Prayer is turning to the resource of divine power. But God will not use His power to help us until we first admit our own inadequacy, our helplessness, our need.

Ray Stedman sounds the same note when he says, "True prayer is an awareness of our helpless need and an acknowledgment of divine adequacy."[6]

As you prepare to pray, think of yourself as a child coming to God your Father. You acknowledge your helplessness. You love your Father and you trust Him. You know He can help and are confident that He will. So you pour out to Him all the concerns that are in your mind and all the burdens of your heart. This kind of talking to God is based on an awareness of His presence and on a trust in His willingness to listen and answer.

4. Be Conscious of the Presence of God

Brother Lawrence, a lay worker in a monastery, sought to develop the habit of practicing in every waking moment of his life what he called "the presence of God." He wanted to be conscious of a personal union with God so that at any time, in the middle of any duty, under any circumstance, he would know that God was with him and that God was aware of whatever need he had and was eager to help. He said, "The time of business does not with me differ from the time of prayer; and in the noise and clutter of my kitchen, while several persons are at the same time calling for different things, I possess God in as great tranquility as if I were on my knees at the blessed sacrament."[7]

The attitude that prepares me to talk to God is the work of the Holy Spirit in my heart. It is an attitude that is conscious of the presence of God every moment, or "moment by moment," as Frank Laubach used to say. As I recognize my need, and seek to reach out to divine help, I know that He is there to hear me and that in His love and concern for me, His child, He will listen to and answer my prayer. That is why I can pray any moment of any day, even if it is merely a sentence prayer, or a "spear thought" sent heavenward. Paul said that we should "pray without ceasing" (1 Thessalonians 5:17). He was suggesting that if God is present every moment of our lives, we can at any moment turn to Him for help in our needs or praise Him for His blessing.

This, of course, takes practice because of all the distractions and the busyness of our lives. When I wake up in the morning and wait for the alarm to go off, I like to focus my thoughts on God, and talk to Him. I say something like this, "Thank you for a new day and for the life and health You give me to live this day. Guide me in all I do and let me bring honor to You." When I go to my desk to begin my day with a quiet time of Scripture and meditation, I turn the calendar on my desk to set the date for the new day and I say in my thoughts something like, "Thank You, for today. I need You to make this Your day and not just mine."

These are some of the ways in which I seek to "practice the presence" of God in my daily life. So when the opportunity or need comes to pray out loud in public, I am aware that God is there and listening, and I can merely continue my talking with Him.

Oscar Feucht in a booklet called *The Practice of Prayer*, said, "Without a doubt, prayer is the greatest art in the world, and a holy art that only needs to be learned. If it is a lost art, it is lost only because man has lost the consciousness of God."[8]

5. Talk in a Personal Way

When you engage in serious conversation with someone you love and trust, your style of conversation is in a manner which is appropriate to your own personality. It does not follow prescribed rules and regulations. It is free expression and moves spontaneously from concern to concern, from one idea to another without necessarily following an organized pattern. This is the way prayer should be, as Hallesby says, "It should be free, spontaneous, vital fellowship between the created person and the personal Creator."[9]

The language of prayer is also personal, using direct, simple, personal words. Some people feel that they should address God in the Elizabethan language that was used in the King James translation of the Bible in 1611 in England, so they speak to God as "Thee" instead of "You," and use "Thy" instead of "Your." Or they use obsolete words and verb endings, "Thou dost love," or "livest and reignest," or "cometh and giveth." People who insist on this language feel that this shows respect and reverence for God. But it should also be said that this language can also make prayers more difficult to understand when read or heard, and it encourages people to think that they have to read prayers that others have written since they do not talk like that.

The prayers recorded in the Bible are in direct, personal language using the same words that were used in everyday conversation with other people. (See Bible Study No. 2 at the end of this chapter.) The prayers of the Bible are more personal than objective, more in the image of a child talking to a father than a servant addressing a king in a formal courtroom. Because of tradition, our ears may be attuned to appreciate the sounds of the psalmist in King James language: "From everlasting to everlasting Thou art God" (Psalm 90:2). Yet the modern words of the Today's English Version are probably more true to the original language and style of Scripture in addressing God: "You were eternally God and will be God forever."

Of course, a person can pray in any language. It is often a matter determined by our experience because we usually like what is familiar to us and what we are accustomed to hearing. In this book, however, the prayers we suggest will be in terms of simple, personal words which address God as "You."

By way of review, we are getting ready to learn how to pray out loud in public by checking our attitude toward prayer so that we have a positive concept of what we are about to do. We need to lay aside some of the habits or customs which hinder us from thinking of praying as coming to God as a child to his father, and talking to Him in a personal way in the language that we are accustomed to using. With that attitude we are ready to discuss specific ways in which to begin to pray. To help you review and elaborate on the thoughts of this chapter, work through the Bible Study and Action section below before you proceed to Chapter 2.

Bible Study and Action

1. Read the story of Jacob at Bethel, Genesis 28:13-22. Find the chief elements of prayer and fill in the blanks:

vs. 13-15 _____

v. 17 _____

vs. 20-22 _____

2. In the Greek language in which the New Testament was written the same words that are used for ordinary "asking" are used for "praying." Here are four such verbs. Each verb is used in the passages listed under it but translated differently in our English versions. Look up the references and compare their use:

deomai: Usually used when presenting a need and is at times translated by "plead" or "beseech."

Matthew 9:38 _____

Luke 5:12 _____

Acts 4:31 _____

Galatians 4:12 _____

parakaleo: The basic meaning is to call to one's aid.

Matthew 5:17 _____

Matthew 26:53 _____

Acts 16:9 _____

eratao: The meaning suggests that the petitioner is on an equal footing.

John 4:31 _____

John 14:16 _____

John 17:9 _____

John 18:19 _____

aiteo: Usually used when a person in a lesser position in life asks some one who is in a higher position, as a child asking his father or a subject asking a king.

Matthew 7:7 _____

Matthew 7:9 _____

Acts 12:20 _____

Ephesians 3:20 _____

3. Read Genesis 18:22-33, an episode in Abraham's relationship with God. Is this a conversation or a prayer? Discuss how these might be the same or how they might be different.

4. Study the two amazing answers to prayer given to King Hezekiah.

    2 Kings 19:14-19: the prayer; 19:20-37: the answer

    2 Kings 20:1-3: the prayer; 20:4-11: the answer

What does the way in which Hezekiah talked to God indicate about his relationship with God?

Chapter 2
P For Praise

Our tour group checked in at the King David Hotel late in the evening. We were in the town of Safed, high in the hills overlooking the Sea of Galilee. Eagerly I asked the hotel manager, "What time does the sun rise? Where can I see the Sea of Galilee from the hill we are on?" I had sufficient information when I went to bed so that I knew exactly what I wanted to do when the alarm went off before daylight the next morning. It was to be a memorable experience.

In the morning, I jogged with my Bible in hand to the designated spot on the edge of town. There I sat on the hillside, watched the sun rise over the Sea of Galilee, and read the Sermon on the Mount. The ground around me was rocky soil with small "lilies" in bloom. In the distance I heard the birds chirp their morning songs. "How many times," I thought, "my Savior must have sat in a place just like this." That verse had always impressed me, but at this moment it took on new meaning. "And in the morning a great while before day, He rose and went out to a lonely place, and there He prayed" (Mark 1:35).

It is easy to pray when one marvels at the beauty of God's creation. And it is easy at that time to begin speaking words of praise and adoration to God. That is how all prayer should start, with praise. Charlie W. Shedd, the well-known author and speaker, in his book describing his own experience, explains *How to Develop a Praying Church*. He suggests that the two essential points of prayer are (1) begin with God, and (2) pray your own way.[1]

If you have worked through Chapter 1, then you should now be ready for more specific directions on how to pray in public. The first point in our four-point acrostic, which comprises the theme for the next chapters, is just that—we begin with God. We begin with praising Him. The four-point prayer acrostic we will follow is:

P is for Praise
R is for Remember
A is for Ask
Y is for Yield

1. Praise Him for Being God

Prayer is talking to our heavenly Father, to present to Him our needs and to ask His help, much as a child speaks to an earthly father. That's what we've said so far. But I think about the kind of God that He is, this person who has become my Father through faith in Jesus Christ. My prayers should start by praising Him for who He is and what He does. Scripture describes Him in so many ways. There are stories about Him, records of His deeds, and simple statements of who He is and what He does. Think of some of the latter:

God is creator of all things in heaven and on earth.

God is eternal—He always was and always will be.

God is almighty with power to heal the sick and raise the dead.

God is holy and perfect and righteous.

God is present everywhere.

God knows all things—past, present, and future.

God does not change. He is the same yesterday, today, and tomorrow.

God is love and mercy, forgiving all sins and iniquity.

As I begin to pray, I come to God as my Father but I think of His majesty and glory, of His love and mercy, of His greatness and goodness, and I praise Him. Rabbi Abraham Joshua Heschel, the noted Jewish theologian and author, said that the essence of prayer is a song.[2] He was thinking of singing our thanks for a world of loveliness. Even though there may be grief and unfairness in the world, the world itself is a place of awesome beauty and wonder. A prayer of praise insists that at the heart of darkness there is an unquenchable light. The Christian can believe that, because he knows what God is like. In all His awesome divinity and power, God is also Light and Love to me. So I praise Him for being God—for being as He is.

The saints and mystics of the church throughout history have placed a great deal of emphasis on praising God for who and what He is. They called this praise adoration. Some of the formulas suggested for learning how to pray use the word "Thanksgiving" as one of the first elements of prayer and include in it both adoration and praise. It is difficult to differentiate today between the words: "adoration," "praise," and "thanks."

In the Psalms, praise is almost like clapping your hands in approval and joy as we do when someone makes a good play in sports. In this way praise does differ from the giving of thanks. "Praise" is used in the Bible twice as often as "thanksgiving" or "thanks."

In order to indicate the difference between the two words "praise" and "thanks," some earlier scholars of the church said that in "praise" my thoughts focus on the majesty and power and grace and love of God, while in "thanks" my thoughts circle around myself and the blessings I receive. Hallesby suggests that the words are so closely akin that "outwardly it is not possible to draw a clear line of demarcation between them. Both consist of giving glory to God."[3] If any distinction can be made, it would be that praise or adoration is giving glory to God for what He is in Himself, and thanks is giving glory to God for what He has done for us. For our purposes it is simpler if we use the word praise to include also thanks and adoration. When I think of praying, I can look at the first letter "P" and start my prayer with praise. I praise God for being God, for what He has done and is doing for me and others, and for His wonderful promises for the future.

2. Praise Him for What He Has Done and Is
   Still Doing

What has He done and what is He still doing? In the past He created this marvelous and awesome universe with all its living creatures including us human beings, and today He preserves that creation and continues to create. But man, the crown of God's creation, rebelled against God and His plan and purpose. However, God in His love reached out to draw mankind back to Himself. He sent His Son to become the substitute for man, taking upon Himself the penalty for the sin of the world, paying that penalty by His death and then rising again from the dead, thus providing peace between man and God. It is said so simply and beautifully in Bible verses like:

John 3:16—God so loved the world that He gave His only Son that whoever believes in Him should not perish but have everlasting life. 2 Corinthians 5:19—In Christ God was reconciling the world to Himself, not counting their trespasses against them.

Praise God for what He has done and also for what He does today! Not only has He reconciled the world, but He has, as Luther put it, "redeemed me a lost and condemned creature," and then "called me by the Gospel, enlightened and sanctified and kept me in the one true faith." Because He has done this "without any merit or worthiness in me," I am a member of His family, and I can come to Him as a child to his father and talk to Him in prayer.

Praise Him for being God. Praise Him for what He has done to make you His child. Praise Him for what He does daily to keep you in faith and protect you from evil. Praise Him for His daily care. Every day He showers blessings on the earth, on others, as well as on you. The old hymn suggests, "Count your blessings, name them one by one." It is impossible to count them all but you can count some of them . . . health, family, work, neighbors, friends, community, nation, church. Too often we magnify our troubles and minimize our blessings. It depends on one's attitude and perspective.

Ardis Whitman learned the hard way. She lost her only son. Wild with grief she raged at God. "Thanks for anything seemed almost a blasphemy," she said. But when she spoke of her anguish to a friend, her friend replied quietly, "I never had a son." As Ardis Whitman remembered that her friend was childless, she learned that a prayer of thanksgiving can accompany even grief as she began to pray many times a day, "Thank you, God, that I have had him."[4]

The example of the saints in Scripture shows us a similar spirit of thanks and praise. The psalmist says, "I will bless the Lord at all times, His praise shall constantly be in my mouth" (Psalm 34:1). St. Paul tells the Christians in Thessalonica, "Give thanks in all circumstances, for this is the will of God in Christ Jesus for you" (1 Thessalonians 5:17-18).

PTL is a popular and familiar exclamation. For some it may stand for Parent Teacher League but today for many it stands for: "Praise the Lord!" Sometimes we say it so glibly. The church triumphant with the "great multitude" in heaven sings special praise to God in their "Hallelujah Chorus." "Hallelujah! Salvation and glory and power belong to our God. . . . His judgments are true and righteous" (Revelation 19:1). "Hallelujah" comes from two Hebrew words which mean "praise" and "Yahweh." From early days the word became a form of public exclamation, combining "the thought of admiration, adulation, and rejoicing."[5] The translation of those Hebrew words to the English "praise the Lord" occurs frequently in the Book of Psalms (Psalm 106; 111; 112; 113; 117; 135; 146—150), though only in Revelation 19 does the word appear in the New Testament.

The very word "psalm" means "song of praise," and we could expect to find, as we do, that the Book of Psalms is full of "praise the Lord" expressions. It is interesting to note that this book of praise is in the center of the Bible, not so much that its location in the 66 books of the Bible is a message from God, but it's central location can serve as a reminder to us that the center of all our Bible reading and prayer should be praise.

3. Praise God for His Promises

As we praise God in our prayers in a general way for all that He is and does, there is one thing for which we should specifically praise Him—His promises. Not only does God encourage, invite, or command us to pray, but He also

promises to hear and answer our prayers. Examine first
some of His invitations to pray:

Isaiah 55:6—Seek the Lord while He may be found,
call upon Him while He is near.

1 Thessalonians 5:17—Pray constantly.

Psalm 50:15—Call upon Me in the day of trouble;
I will deliver you, and you shall glorify Me.

The invitations or commands to pray are often connected with the promises that God gives us to hear and
answer our prayers. Here are a few of them:

Matthew 7:7—Ask, and it will be given you; seek,
and you will find; knock, and it will be opened to
you.

Psalm 9:15—When he calls to Me, I will answer him;
I will be with him in trouble, I will rescue him and
honor him.

Isaiah 65:24—Before they call I will answer, while
they are yet speaking I will hear.

John 15:7—Ask whatever you will, and it shall be
done for you.

Luke 11:9-10—Ask, and it will be given you; seek,
and you will find; knock, and it will be opened to
you. For everyone who asks receives, and he who
seeks finds, and to him who knocks it will be opened.

We will discuss later answers to prayer, but as we begin
praying, it is important that we praise God for His promises
and trust them as we bring our needs and wants to Him.
That is the conviction that is expressed when we sing the
ancient doxology of the church:

Praise God from whom all blessings flow;
Praise Him all creatures here below;
Praise Him above, ye heavenly host;
Praise Father, Son, and Holy Ghost.

4. Put Praise into Words

But our praise must be more specific and more personal
than singing the above doxology in church once a week—or
once a month. One way that we become more specific is in

the custom of thanking God for His blessings every time we sit down to eat a meal, whether in the privacy of our home or in a public restaurant. Some Christians follow the tradition of reciting memorized words like "Come, Lord Jesus, be our guest . . . " or "For health and strength and daily food we praise Thy name, O Lord . . . . " Other Christians enjoy making their own prayers when they share a meal with someone else. One person is asked to pray out loud and compose a prayer that is specific to that situation.

In his book, *Life Sentence*, Charles Colson tells of going to a restaurant with his friend.[6] Fred prayed out loud. When the two of them raised their heads, the waitress was standing there waiting for them to finish. "Hey, were you guys praying?" she asked. She spoke so loud that everyone in the small room turned to look. "Yes," Colson replied. "Hey, that's neat," the waitress went on. "I've never seen anybody do that in here before. Are you preachers?" "No, not really. But we work in the same business," Colson answered.

That led to a lengthy conversation in which the waitress admitted that she had been a Christian once, when she was a teenager, but that she had lost interest. "Funny thing," she said, "a girl friend of mine has been wanting me to go to a Bible study group with her." And she added thoughtfully, "I think I will!"

Suppose that you were Fred, and Charles Colson had asked you to lead in prayer. How would you start? Think of the acrostic? PRAY—"P for praise." Now add to that "Praise God for being God," and think of all that we have said about who God is and what He does.

But before you launch into general praise of God, think about the situation, the occasion, the need at the moment. You and Charles Colson are talking about prison ministry and some of the problems confronted in getting permission to hold seminars in federal prisons. That gives you some cues as to how to address God and what to praise Him for as you begin to connect the needs of the situation to what you know about God.

Perhaps you could start praying like this:

> Gracious Father, I praise You that You are the Lord
> of all institutions and that You love prisoners just as
> You love Charles and me . . .

and then you go on to R and A and Y in the acrostic.

Suppose you are in a different situation. Suppose you are visiting a sick friend and as you prepare your thought for prayer you think of God as Father in that situation. You might say:

> God, as a Father, You are concerned for Your
> children when they are sick. I thank and praise You
> for Your care and especially that You are a God who
> gives strength and comfort and You heal when it is
> in Your will . . .

Suppose you are asked to open a Lion's Club meeting with prayer. You think of "P for Praise" in terms of your community or the meal you will share, the fellowship around the tables, or the business to be done. You might then speak to God as the Lord of the nations, the Giver of all gifts, and praise Him for the opportunity to be there together with the others on that occasion.

There is no set formula, or one right way, to begin a prayer. It is helpful to think of God as both the almighty Creator and Lord and as my Father, and then in the opening words praise Him for His involvement in the present moment. Some people may prefer to think of Jesus as the Son of God and address their prayers to Him as their Friend or their Savior and Lord. The popular hymn, "What a Friend We Have in Jesus," may have encouraged that kind of praying. The hymn, however, doesn't picture Jesus as the one to whom we pray. Remember the line, "What a privilege to carry, everything to God in prayer." Jesus is the one who has born our "sins and griefs" on the cross and, because He has, we can come to God, as children of the family of God, and "take it to the Lord in prayer." Jesus promised: "What you ask the Father in My name, He will give it to you" (John 16:23).

This does not mean that we cannot address our prayers to Jesus, for He is truly the Son of God, the Lord before

whom every knee will bow (Philippians 2:11), but it seems more conducive to personal conversation to think of talking to God as my Father. Martin Luther emphasized that when you pray, "no matter which person you call upon, you call upon all three Persons and upon the One God at the same time. For you cannot call upon one Person without calling upon the others, because the one, undivided divine Essence exists in all and in each Person."[7]

In this chapter, we have examined the first letter in the word PRAY, P for Praise, and have suggested that we "Praise God for being God." With our thoughts focused on God, the Almighty, who is our Father, we speak to Him as children speak to their father. We praise Him in terms of the specific time and place where we are praying. This can help our self-consciousness when we pray in public context. Our thoughts center on God and not on what the people around us think of us or our words. Our desire to praise Him crowds out our fear of the judgment of others.

Now work through the Bible Study and Action section which follows to further think through the opening greeting or address of your prayer and how to begin with praise.

Bible Study and Action

1. Read Acts 1:24-26 and fill in the blanks.

   How did they address God? _____

   How did they describe God? _____

   What was their request? _____

2. Read Acts 4:24-31

   How did they address God? _____

   How did they describe what God had done? _____

32

What did they ask? _____

3. In the greetings in Paul's letters, he wished his readers "grace and peace." From whom does this "grace and peace" come according to Paul"

Romans 1:7 _____

1 Corinthians 1:3 _____

2 Corinthians 1:2 _____

Colossians 1:2 _____

What is the significance of joining the two words "God" and "Father?"

4. Read Psalm 150 (you might also read Psalms 146—149).

Who should praise the Lord? _____

Where should we praise the Lord? _____

For what should we praise the Lord? _____

With what should we praise the Lord? _____

5. Read some printed prayers in a hymnbook or in a prayer book. Make a list of the words used to address God and the words used to praise and thank Him.

_____   _____

_____   _____

_____   _____

6. If God were visible and sitting with you right now, how would you address Him and what would you say to praise or thank Him? List some examples:

Words of Address: _____

_____

Words of Thanks and Praise: _____

_____

Chapter 3
R for Remember

The fellows are all gathered around the telephone booth while Frank places a call to Diane, the school beauty queen. Frank starts talking into the receiver as his friends watch through the glass. They can only imagine what is being said. Frank is determined to impress his buddies with his ability to get a date with Diane, or any girl he wants. After a while, Frank hangs up the telephone and walks past his friends with a Cheshire cat grin that is intended to tell the story of success.

But that's not quite the whole story. Actually, Frank got a busy signal when he tried to call Diane, but he went ahead and faked the conversation. Diane wasn't on the line at all.[1] In one sense, we can compare prayer to a telephone call to our Father in heaven. But with Him there is no such thing as a busy signal. He is always on the line waiting for His children to talk to Him. We said in the last chapter that when we begin to pray to our Father, we do so with praise, P for Praise, praise Him for being God, for who He is, what He has done and continues to do.

When I lie in bed at night and sleep does not immediately come or when I awake in the middle of the night and wait for sleep to return, I talk to my Father in my thoughts. It used to be that the talk was more like reciting a catalog of requests, help me do this, give me that, or at times it was praying for family and friends, reviewing the needs of each one in turn and asking my Father to help each need. However, as I developed the acrostic on the word PRAY, I was reminded that I needed to begin my praying with thanks and praise to God for what He had already done and continues to do in my life and what He does for all my loved ones and friends. Now when I roll and toss, I also praise God, recalling what kind of an infinite, almighty, and all-knowing God He is; and in such recall I am often overwhelmed by the majesty, wisdom, and power of God when compared to my weak, sinful and mortal, human nature. This emphasized for me the need to follow up my "P for Praise" with the second letter in the acrostic, "R for Remember," remember who I am.

1. Remember Who You Are

It was in this way that the second line of our verse on the acrostic of the word PRAY developed, as I remembered who I was. In order to put that into the same kind of direction for learning how to pray in public that is used in the first line, we need to change the wording so that it is addressed to you, the reader. Then it comes out like this:

P for Praise—Praise God for Who He Is and What He Does.
R for Remember—Remember Who You Are.

When we remember who we are, two things stand out clearly from the pages of Scripture, that we are mortal and that we are sinful. Recognizing and accepting this set prepares us for praying. We are mortal human beings coming into the presence of an eternal and immortal God. We are sinful beings, coming before a holy and righteous Lord. We can only come in a spirit of humility and confession seeking forgiveness. It is through confession and forgiveness that the way is cleared and we have open access to approach our Father with our needs. This is what Maxie Dunnam calls "clearing the channel"[2] so that there can be open communication with the Almighty.

In a similar vein in his book, the *Struggle of Prayer*, Donald Bloesch says that the all-powerful and all-knowing God hears and knows all prayer, but as the Holy One, He detests all sin and iniquity, and He "will not give an open ear to prayers that arise out of human arrogance and give glory only to man. The throne of God must therefore be approached in fear and trembling born out of the recognition that God is infinite and holy, whereas we are finite and sinful."[3]

In Chapter 2 we focused our attention on God, but in

this chapter we focus our thoughts on ourselves, looking in depth at those two truths, "we are finite (or mortal), and we are sinful."

2. Remember—You Are Mortal

In the beginning God said, "Let there be light" (Genesis 1:3), and "there was light." For six days God said, "Let there be," and the universe was created and inhabited. God also said on the sixth day, "Let us make man . . . " (Genesis 1:26). There is no doubt in that creation account in Genesis 1 who the Creator was, or who is the Lord of creation. The opening verse says, "In the beginning God" (Genesis 1:1). It doesn't try to explain where God came from or who He was. He was always there as the ultimate, eternal being. He was and is immortal.

But the world and every living thing in it is mortal. Neither the earth nor the creature will last forever; both are constantly changing and will someday be destroyed. The God who said, "Let Us make man," some time later said, "I will blot out man whom I have created from the face of the ground" (Genesis 6:7). And He did just that with a flood that covered the whole world with water, even to the depth of 22 feet above the peak of Mt. Everest! (Genesis 7:20). The only living creatures not destroyed were the members of Noah's family, whom God decided to save by means of the Ark, and one pair of each of the animals and birds. After it was over, God said, "neither will I ever again destroy every living creature" (Genesis 8:21).

Had anything changed in man? He had rebelled against God and had become selfish and evil. That was why God destroyed him. But why did God decide to destroy man and then after the flood promise never again to destroy him? Before the flood, Scripture describes man like this: "The wickedness of man was great . . . and every imagination of the thoughts of his heart was only evil continually" (Genesis 6:5). After the flood a similar expression is used, "the imagination of man's heart is evil from his youth" (Genesis 8:21). What had changed? Not man. God demonstrated His love and mercy. Now He would show man the way of salvation He had told to Adam and Eve already in the Garden of Eden. Through His Son, God would provide a way of escape from the evil of his own heart so that man could return to the kind of fellowship with God that was intended for His original creation.

That is what the whole New Testament story of the life, death, and resurrection of Jesus Christ is about. Now God offers to man the free gift of eternal life, rather than destroying him with a flood because of his evil (Romans 6:23).

When we come to God in prayer, we remember that we are mortal, human beings that God created and that He can destroy. If we think of all the aches and pains in our bodies, the sickness and aging, the weakness and failings of our minds and bodies as signs of our mortality, we begin to realize how we need the immortal God. We need one who never changes but continues to be the almighty and loving Lord who is without "variation or shadow due to change" (James 1:17). Remember how the psalmist said it:

A thousand years in Thy sight are but as yesterday when it is past, or as a watch in the night (Psalm 90:4).

Thou dost sweep men away; they are like a dream, like grass which is renewed in the morning: In the morning it flourishes and is renewed; in the evening it fades and withers (Psalm 90:5-6).

Of old Thou didst lay the foundation of the earth, and the heavens are the work of Thy hands. They will perish, but Thou dost endure; they will wear out like a garment. Thou changest them like raiment, and they pass away; but Thou art the same, and Thy years have no end (Psalm 102:25-27).

R is for Remember. Remember who you are—you are mortal.

3. Remember—You Are a Sinner

I was at a Women's Missionary League retreat where

we talked about "putting on" the fruit of the Spirit on the basis of Colossians 3 and Galatians 5—love, joy, peace, compassion, kindness, and all the rest. During the free time, one lady came up to me and said, "I think we should stop talking so much about sin. That doesn't help us put on the fruit of the Spirit. It's too negative."

I was somewhat surprised and asked her what she meant. "Well," she said, "why do we have to say every Sunday in our liturgy, 'I, a poor miserable sinner.' I don't feel that way when I say it. I live for God day by day, and I don't commit any major crimes."

"It helps me appreciate God's grace," I reasoned, "to remember what kind of a person I really am underneath the surface, a sinful and selfish being who is subject to all the temptations of the devil and who does commit actual sins every day more often than is realized. It also helps to remember that God just keeps forgiving and forgetting them over and over again."

When we talk to God in prayer, it is helpful to remember who we are—sinners. Because of our corrupted human nature, we are sinful and do commit sins. One of the root words for sin in the Bible is "missing the mark," missing the purpose of God's intentions for us and the standard He gives by which He wants us to live. It is as if a man, one who is highly trained in the skill of space flight and exploration, trained at tremendous cost of time and money, spent his life riding a merry-go-round. God created me to live in fellowship with Him, to live a life that is in harmony with His will and His commandments. Sin is defined as missing that purpose. It is breaking or transgressing God's will. It is rebelling against Him.

The Bible describes my condition in a number of dramatic ways. The psalmist David says that I inherited a sinful nature, which theologians call original or inherited sin:

Behold I was brought forth in iniquity, and in sin did
my mother conceive me (Psalm 51:5).

Some people in the past have used those words to teach

that sexual intercourse, even in marriage, is sinful. But that is not what David means. The words say that from the moment of my conception on I was sinful. It is because of that basic nature that Ecclesiastes says, "Surely there is not a righteous man on earth who does good and never sins" (Ecclesiastes 7:20). Isaiah summarizes our sinful mortal condition by saying:

> We have all become like one who is unclean, and all our righteous deeds are like a polluted garment. We all fade like a leaf, and our iniquities, like the wind, take us away (Isaiah 64:6).

Maxie Dunnam says it well: "Sin is not only what we do, it is often what we think and are. It is our separation from God, our failure to live in obedient relationship to Him." She uses a phrase from the book, *Cloud of Unknowing*, saying that sometimes we feel like a "lump of sin," which she describes by saying that "our inner-being seems out-of-joint, out of relationship with God. We don't feel any oneness. Our lives are fragmented, out of focus."[4]

How can we get back into that original relationship with God in which we know our "oneness," so that we can talk to Him as a child talks to its loving father?

As sin brings separation, so confession opens the door to communion. Remembering our sinful nature as well as our actual sins, we come to God and confess our specific failures to do His will and the specific sins which we remember, knowing that unless we confess and receive forgiveness, those sins result in death. A man read the Bible verse on the bulletin board in front of a church, "The wages of sin is death," and he muttered to himself as he walked on, "That's one price that hasn't gone up." It can't go any higher. Or any lower either. God's promise is, "If we confess our sins, He is faithful and just, and will forgive our sins and cleanse us from all unrighteousness" (1 John 1:9). Then John says we have fellowship with the Father and with His Son Jesus Christ. Then the "channel is clear." We can talk to God, confident that He will hear and answer.

4. Remember—What Is "Proper Prayer"

As we approach God to talk to Him, we remember who we are—sinful mortals coming into the presence of a holy, immortal God, and we realize our need for forgiveness. Assured of that forgiveness, we now begin to pour out our needs without stopping to say, "Is this the proper attitude in which to pray?" Yet occasionally it is good to review what the Bible teaches about how to pray, or what some prefer to call a "proper prayer." This is a good place for us to do that in this book as we talk about remembering—remembering what is a proper prayer. We can summarize the Bible teaching on what is a "proper prayer" with these four statements: (1) Pray in the name of Jesus, (2) Pray with confidence, (3) Pray according to God's will, and (4) Pray in the Spirit. The first two of these points we will discuss now; the remaining two will be covered in the final chapter.

a. Pray in the Name of Jesus

Most prayers, both printed ones and *ex corde* prayers, end with the phrase "in the name of Jesus," "for Jesus' sake," or a similar phrase. It is natural that Christians would develop this kind of practice, for Jesus told us to pray in His name and to ask things for His sake. Although no prayers in the Bible use these expressions, Christians were at times baptized "in the name of the Lord Jesus" (Acts 2:38; 8:16; 19:5). These customs of ending a prayer with the words, "in the name of Jesus," or a similar expression, developed later as Christians remembered the words of Jesus, as in the King James translation, "Whatsoever ye shall ask the Father in My name, He will give it you" (John 16:23). Modern translations alter the sequence in that verse and connect "in My name" with "give it to you." In other passages Jesus said:

Whatever you ask in My name, I will do it (John 14:13).

If you ask anything in My name, I will do it (John 14:14).

Christians took that phrase out of the Bible and attached it to their prayers to indicate that they were praying as Jesus said they should. But, unfortunately, doing that can become misleading.

A college student came to me one day after a chapel devotion which I had led. He was rather upset and said, "That wasn't a Christian prayer you used today!" He insisted that to be a Christian prayer, a prayer had to have the phrase, "in the name of Jesus," or a similar expression, at the end. That is not what Jesus meant when he said that we should ask in His name. "In the name of" means in His authority, on the basis of Him. (Cf. Colossians 3:17.) He meant that it is because of Him that we receive the forgivenss of sins and are able to come into the presence of God. It is through His name that we come into the relationship of a child to its heavenly Father. It is in that forgivenss that we have the privilege to pray. If we no longer live in the forgiving grace of God, we cannot pray with the assurance of God's promise to hear and answer (Psalm 66:18-19). To close our prayer "in the name of Jesus" is a reminder to us that we need to trust in Him and that it is only through Him that we come to God. But we can be in that relationship of a forgiven child of God through faith in Jesus without actually saying the words "in the name of Jesus." The Lord's Prayer does not conclude with the words "in the name of Jesus."

b. Pray with Confidence

The second Bible teaching about "proper prayer" is that we pray with confidence, which is described in the explanation to Luther's *Small Catechism*, "that is, with firm trust that for Jesus' sake our prayer will be answered."[5]
The Bible speaks about praying in confidence with words like this:

> Let him ask in faith, with no doubting, for he who doubts is like a wave of the sea that is driven and tossed by the wind. For that person must not suppose that a double-minded man, unstable in all his ways, will receive anything from the Lord (James 1:6-7).

42

Therefore, I tell you, whatever you ask in prayer, believe that you have received it, and it will be yours (Mark 11:24).

Praying with confidence or with faith means that we are sure God will keep His promises. Prayer is not so much a matter of feeling that God is close, that He loves us and will be good to us, as it is relying on the promises He has given. There are times when I experience what I suspect most Christians experience from time to time, a dryness or emptiness in my spiritual life. At those times I am tempted to complain, "When I try to pray, I don't feel anything." Or I want to cry out, "God, are You there? Why don't You give me some assurance, some indication that I can know You are listening to me." I am strengthened, when those temptations come, by remembering the promises of God, and I put my trust not on my feelings but on those promises.

Lois Walfrid Johnson described in her book, *Either Way, I Win,* how she struggled with this same problem. She tells of growing in prayer as she discovered that she had cancer, and went through a mastectomy and chemotherapy treatments with all the side effects. As the dosage was increased during the months on chemotherapy, she says that the "joy and sense of aliveness I normally experienced diminished, leaving me feeling dead inside." During that time, she was sustained by pinning a sentence on the curtain above the kitchen sink where she could see it often: "The Christian life is a walk of faith, not of feelings."[6] Prayer in the same way is not a matter of feelings but of faith, of trusting confidently in the promises of God to forgive us, to hear us and to answer our prayers.

5. Remember a Theme for Prayer

R for remember—remember who you are, a sinful, mortal human being. Remember that a proper prayer means praying with confidence in the name of Jesus. When we discussed in the last chapter the first letter of our prayer acrostic, P for Praise, we suggested that it is helpful for our praise to remember the occasion where we are praying, so that we can thank and praise God for specific items related to that event or organization or people. The same may be said for the second letter in the acrostic which we have discussed in this chapter, R for Remember, as well as for the rest of the acrostic which we will discuss in the next chapters—A for Ask and Y for Yield.

As your thoughts focus on the occasion of when and where you are praying, remember the failures and sins related to that occasion. For example, continue the prayer that we started in the last chapter when we suggested that you imagine Charles Colson talking with you about prison ministry:

Gracious Father, I praise You that You are the Lord of all institutions and that You love prisoners just as You love me and Charles.

Now R for remember, remember who you are:

We are all constantly tempted to sin and I have done my share. I so often have judged the motives of those who are caught committing a crime, and I have wanted to see them pay for their wrong. Forgive my lack of compassion, my failure to help prevent crime, and my reluctance to visit those in prison . . . .

Or take the prayer started in the last chapter as we envisioned a visit to a sick friend.

God, as a Father, You are concerned for Your children when they are sick. I thank and praise You for Your care and especially that You are a God who gives strength and comfort and healing when it is in Your will . . . .

Now R for Remember, remember who you are:

We are so human and mortal that we need Your daily care and the strength You give. So often, Father, I fail to look to You for health and I trust only the doctor for healing. Forgive me for my worrying and lack of faith . . . .

The occasion for our prayer in these two examples gives us a theme for our prayer. That theme, however, can be

more than just the occasion at which we are praying. We might add, for instance, the season of the church year, or some special holiday. For example, the occasion for my prayer might be the opening of a meeting at church of the men's group or women's group. If it is the Lenten season of the church year, my prayer might include specific references to the suffering and death of Jesus Christ. Or if it is near the Fourth of July, I might include thoughts about living in a free land. Again the subject matter to be studied or discussed at a particular meeting might suggest the theme for my prayer.

Suppose that you are asked to open the meeting with prayer as the leaders of your church are meeting to plan a parish program for the coming year. Your prayer could proceed like this. Although we have not yet discussed the "A for Ask" and the "Y for Yield," we are including paragraphs on those subjects in this prayer in order to complete this illustration as a complete prayer.

P for Praise:

> Dear Father, You are the Lord of the church, and by Your Spirit You direct and guide it; we thank You for the blessings You continue to give so graciously to Your church, not only Your daily care and forgiveness but pastoral leadership and the willing lay people gathered here.

R for Remember:

> We confess that we so often take Your blessings for granted, and don't thank You for them. At times we are lazy and indifferent in the use of the gifts and the opportunities that You give us for service to Your church.

A for Ask:

> Forgive us, gracious Father. Renew us with Your Spirit. We ask that You continue to bless Your church, and that You would be present in a special way in this meeting to guide our thoughts and planning, that all our plans may be according to Your will and may bring glory to Your name. Give

us faith to set challenging goals and use them to build Your kingdom.

Y for Yield:
> We surrender our own desires and preferences now to You as we seek Your will for Your church. Move us and all our members to participate wholeheartedly, each fulfilling his or her particular function in the body of Christ. Hear us, Father, as we come to You in Jesus' name. Amen.

That prayer may be too long for you to use, but some of the thoughts in it could be in your prayer, either written out ahead of time, or prayed at the moment, *ex corde*. Why not practice right now by composing your own prayer. Either write a prayer in this book or write the headings on a blank sheet of paper and put the parts of your prayer after them. At the very least, if you are reluctant to write a prayer, compose a prayer in your thoughts. We haven't yet discussed the "A for Ask" and the "Y for Yield," but they are added here for the sake of completeness. You may want to wait with that part of your prayer until you read the chapters on those subjects. We learn to pray by praying!

The Occasion: _____

The Theme: _____

P for Praise:
> (Praise God for who He is and what He has done, related to the occasion or theme.)

R for Remember:
> (Remember that you are a mortal, sinful human. Confess specific failures and sins.)

A for Ask:
> (Ask for personal needs and the needs of others.)

Y for Yield:
(Yield to the will of God and to service in His kingdom.)

Bible Study and Action

1. Read Psalm 51 and fill in the blanks below and answer the following questions:

    a. List the words used to address and describe God: __

    _____

    b. What expressions indicate that David thought of himself as a "lump of sin": _____

    _____

    c. What does David ask God to do with his sins? What does he then promise God: _____

    _____

2. The Bible speaks about hindrances that prevent our prayers from being heard or answered. They might be called "short circuits" in our prayer line. Read the following passages and list in each case the reason for the short circuit.

    Proverbs 1:24-29 _____

    Isaiah 59:1-2 _____

    Luke 11:5-9 _____

    James 1:5-8 _____

    James 4:3 _____

    1 Peter 3:7 _____

3. One of the weaknesses of many of our prayers is vagueness on our part as to what we should confess. Think of what you have done the past 24 hours. Make a list of specific sins which you need to confess and specific temptations which trouble you.

Psalm 66:18 _____

James 5:16 _____

4. In the book *What Happens When Women Pray*, Evelyn Christenson[7] lists (pages 24-25) the following sins which she and her partners in prayer discovered when they confronted the need to confess their sins. Are these sins prominent in your life? Add to the list:
   Superior attitude—because of spiritual status
   Divided motives—for serving Christ
   Pretense—being less than honest with God and others
   Pride—"Look what I've done!"

_____

_____

5. The New Testament speaks about Jesus as our "Advocate" with the Father. It says that "He intercedes for us." Examine these passages:

Romans 8:34 _____

1 John 2:1 _____

Does Jesus' "advocating" or "interceding" refer only to our forgiveness and acceptance by the Father or does it include more? Does this put any more meaning in the truth that we pray "in the name of Jesus?"

Chapter 4
A for Ask

"Prayer is something deeper than words. It is present in the soul before it has been formulated in words. And it abides in the soul after the last words of prayer have passed over our lips,"[1] so writes Hallesby in his book on prayer. To which we say, "Amen! But . . . "

"Prayer is to the soul what breath is to the body"[2] is an often used comparison. As the human body needs to breathe air so as to fill the lungs with the oxygen needed to clean impurities out of the system, so the spiritual life of the soul needs by praying to inhale life from God and to exhale the impurities that would destroy it. To which we say, "Amen! But . . . "

Prayer is more than presenting to God a "want list." It is begging His help in need. It is also praising and thanking, confessing and seeking forgiveness. Again we heartily agree with all who say these things by adding our "Amen!" and yet also adding our "But . . . "

What is the "But . . . " all about? After we have said all the things mentioned above about prayer, we come to the heart of the matter, that is, talking to someone with whom we have a personal relationship. In words and thoughts, we talk to God as a child talks to its Father, in direct, honest, specific words. In our talk we praise and confess, we ask Him for His help in our needs and for the needs of others. The popular explanation to Luther's *Small Catechism* summarizes it well when it defines prayer like this: "Prayer is an act of worship wherein we bring our *petitions* before God with our *hearts and lips* and offer up *praise* and *thanksgiving* to Him."[3] (Italics by the author) So we come to the third letter in our acrostic on prayer, *A* is for *Ask*, and we build our acrostic by adding the phrase for "ask":

Praise God for being God.

Remember who you are.
Ask what you want.

1. Ask for Personal Needs

What do we ask for? What kind of petitions do we bring? We say "Ask what you want!" Isn't that audacious on our part? Is there no limit or control on what is proper to ask for? Is God really concerned about all our petty problems and tiny troubles? We can and should ask for whatever we want because Jesus said, "If you abide in Me, and My words abide in you, ask *whatever you will,* and it shall be done for you" (John 15:7). There is no control or limit in that!

Just as a child talks to its father freely and confidently about such things as the scab on his knee, the mean boy next door, or the dream of some day being a great doctor, so the child of God can talk to his heavenly Father about his day-to-day personal needs and concerns as well as the desires and dreams of the heart. Nothing is too small nor too big for our Father to be concerned about and to give His help. The hymn writer encourages us to bring our every need to God, no matter how impossible that need may seem:

Thou art coming to a King,
Large petitions with thee bring,
For His grace and power are such,
None can ever ask too much.
—John Newton, 1779, *TLH* 459

Yes even the little things are of concern to our Father. Because of our friend, Jesus, who opens the way for us to come to His Father and ours, we can come with "everything":

What a Friend we have in Jesus
All our sins and griefs to bear!
What a privilege to carry
Everything to God in prayer!
Oh, what peace we often forfeit,
Oh, what needless pain we bear,
All because we do not carry
Everything to God in prayer!
—Joseph Scriven, 1865, *TLH* 457

a. Spiritual Needs, First

"Everything to God in prayer," but there are some priorities. In the Lord's Prayer Jesus teaches us to give priority to spiritual matters. There are seven "petitions" or "askings" in the prayer Jesus gave when His disciples asked Him to teach them to pray. He said, "When you pray, pray like this . . . " After the address, "Our Father," He tells us to make three distinctly spiritual requests: "Hallowed be Thy name," "Thy kingdom come," "Thy will be done." Only then would He have us ask for physical blessings. This is a pattern, a model for us to follow. That is why some people have suggested that what we call "The Lord's Prayer" should rather be called "The Disciples' Prayer." The real Lord's Prayer, or an example of how our Lord prayed, is in John 17, the prayer of Jesus for His church. What we call "The Lord's Prayer" is really the prayer which is to serve as our model when we pray.[4]

As we continue to compose our prayers with the acrostic: P for Praise, R for Remember, we come to A for Ask! Now we ask what we want, and those wants or concerns should focus first on our spiritual needs and then on the spiritual needs of others. We think of the church on earth, our friends and family, the will of God that all people on earth come to repentance (2 Peter 3:9), and of the commission that He has given to make disciples of all nations of the earth (Matthew 28:19-20). The list of spiritual needs goes on and on. In different prayers on different occasions we bring them all to our Father as specific requests.

b. Physical Needs, Second

Now let's look at that one petition or asking phrase in the model "Lord's Prayer" that speaks about our physical needs. Remember its place among all the petitions. It follows the three petitions that deal with spiritual needs and in turn is followed by three that speak about "forgiveness, temptation, and evil"; and these are really related to our spiritual needs of the first three petitions. The petition that deals with our physical needs merely says, "Give us this day our daily bread." Of course, as Dr. Luther emphasizes in his explanation of this petition, God gives us our daily bread without asking for it. This petition is to remind us that all our physical needs are filled by God on a daily basis—as we need them—and to be received—as we learn daily—with thanksgiving.

When we speak about "daily bread," we need to make sure our thinking includes, as Luther tells us in his explanation to that petition: "Everything that belongs to the support and wants of the body, such as food, drink, clothing, shoes, house, home, field, cattle, money, goods, a pious spouse, pious children, pious servants, pious and faithful rulers, good government, good weather, peace, health, discipline, honor, good friends, faithful neighbors, and the like." What a model this is for us in praying about our physical needs! Luther's words should stimulate our thoughts to our own specific needs in our modern, complicated, economic world. Instead of "field, cattle, money and goods," we might think of our job, the rent, car payment, and heating bill; instead of "pious servants" it may be "an understanding boss or a faithful secretary."

A is for Ask, asking God for all the things that we need, both spiritual and physical, no matter how insignificant or how enormous they may be. If they are needs, God our Father invites us to bring them to Him in prayer. But our asking should not stop with our own needs.

2. Ask for the Needs of Others

Asking God for personal needs is the natural place to begin to "ask what you want," but we must go on to the second step to ask for the needs of others. The famous preacher Edmund McKendree Bounds once said, "Talking to men for God is a great thing, but talking to God for men is greater still."[5]

Sometimes theologians make a distinction between "petition" or "supplication" and "intercession," defining "petition" and "supplication" as asking or presenting to God a specific request for oneself, and "intercession" as bringing a request for someone else. Regardless of our definition, whether we speak of "intercession" or just "asking for others," the Bible strongly encourages praying for others. It gives many examples of how the early church did this. Read this Scripture:

> Pray all the time. Ask God for anything in line with the Holy Spirit's wishes. Plead with Him, reminding Him of your needs, and *keep praying earnestly for all Christians everywhere. Pray for me* too, and ask God to give me the right words as I boldly tell others about the Lord.
>
> —Ephesians 6:18-19 (The Living Bible)

> *We always pray for you,* that our God may make you worthy of His call, and may fulfill every good resolve and work of faith by His power.
>
> —2 Thessalonians 1:11

> Confess your sins to one another, and *pray for one another,* that you may be healed. The prayer of a righteous man has great power in its effects.
>
> —James 5:16

It is easy to say, "Pray for others." It is another matter to incorporate a daily concern for others in our prayer life. While Charlie Shedd, the well-known author and columnist, was minister of Memorial Drive Presbyterian Church in Houston, Texas, he determined with his church leaders that one of their goals would be to make their church a "house of prayer," in keeping with Jesus' statement in Matthew 21:13, "My house shall be called a house of prayer." For them this meant to develop a program which would organize the membership in such a way that each member was prayed for daily by someone in the congregation. They accomplished this through 250 undershepherds who daily were assigned to various kinds of groups—special interest prayer groups, groups for intercession, high school prayer groups, and a study group for continued growth. The undershepherds daily prayed for each person in the group to which he was assigned. As a result, Pastor Shedd says that homes were saved, attitudes were changed, old problems resolved, unhealthy emotions healed, and new souls were reached.[6]

Ask on behalf of *others*. These *others* may be the members of your own church. Do so in either an organized or an unorganized program. The *others* may also be your relatives, or neighbors, or friends. Keep them on a prayer list that notes the special concerns of each one for whom you decide to pray. One friend of mine takes the membership list of his congregation and throughout the year prays in turn for each member whose name is on the list. There are many ways to help us remember to pray for other people and other concerns, but we need to find a way and adapt it to suit our style of life and manner of prayer. Whichever way you choose, be sure to pray for specific needs. Don't be satisfied with a general "bless all my friends and relatives."

The World Mission Prayer League published a tract-booklet on "How to Pray for Your Missionary" in which 16 pages are devoted to suggesting specifics for which to pray, such as: intellectual growth, physical health, positive mental attitude, compassion, help in overcoming fatigue, and developing spiritual maturity. Even those general areas of prayer concern should become more specific and personal. The author of that tract-booklet, Karen Merkel, relates how satisfying it was to know that, during her furlough on which she had a bout with cancer, surgery, and cobalt treatment, she was "bathed in prayer support from so many." But four months later when she was back in La Paz, Bolivia, she was overcome with depression as an aftershock of her experience. This was when she especially needed the assurance that she was still on the prayer list of her supporters.[7]

Pray for *others*, and be specific in those prayers. How often have you said to a friend in need, "I'll pray for you"? Did you really pray for that person? I must confess that I have often said the same thing or written it on a get-well card or sympathy card, and have then forgotten about the matter entirely. As I became more sensitive to praying for others, this began to bother me. My conscience would remind me that I told that person I would pray and I hadn't done it! So I developed a custom that instead of writing on a card, "I will pray for you," I write, "I am praying for you." And I do pray for that person while I write the card and prepare it for mailing, and I continue to pray for him throughout that day in my thoughts. Then if it is a serious need I write that person's name on my prayer list and keep it in my Bible to associate it with my daily reading of God's Word.

Cecil Murphey in his book, *Prayerobics,* relates how he handles a situation when someone asks him to pray for him. He asks, "What do you want me to pray for? Your general mental attitude? Your ability to work?" He says, "I find it easier to pray when I ask God for specific things." He tells of a friend, Larry, who responded to his questions by asking him to pray for his moods of depression. Murphey promised to do so. He said, "For the next month I intend to pray for you every single day. At the end of that time, I will stop unless I hear from you to continue."[8] That is a prayer contract, which is necessary if I am going to be serious about praying for others. I need to know what to pray for and how long to pray.

Another help in learning how to pray for others is to use the printed prayer lists which some magazines and journals publish, or which some organizations send to their prayer supporters. These lists often suggest a prayer concern for each day of the month. By adding these concerns to my personal prayer list, I have the satisfaction of knowing that I am praying not only for my friends and those whom I know personally, but also the larger needs of the church, and the concerns of world evangelization.

Developing the habit of praying for others, through whatever kind of prayer lists or other program that you use, can help you become conscious of the needs of others. This can become a means of growing in your prayer life and a help in composing prayers when you pray in public.

3. Ask with Others

A for Ask, Ask what you want, what you want for

yourself and what you want for others. To this might be added another dimension of asking which is to ask *with* others, as well as *for* them. Jesus suggested that there was special blessing if His followers would agree to pray together for a need:

If two of you agree on earth about anything they ask, it will be done for them by My Father in heaven. For where two or three are gathered in My name, there am I in the midst of them. Matthew 18:19-20

The Book of Acts records that group prayer was an essential ingredient in the life of the early church. We read that immediately after the Ascension, while the disciples waited for the fulfillment of the promise of the Spirit, "they devoted themselves to prayer together with the women and Mary the mother of Jesus, and with his brothers" (Acts 1:14). Or as the Today's English Version paraphrases it, they "joined together in a group to pray frequently." In Acts 4 after the apostles were released from prison, they went to the home of some friends, and in that home they all prayed together (Acts 4:23-31). When Peter was put in prison by Herod, believers met in homes to pray for him. When he was miraculously released from prison and went to the house of Mary, the mother of John, there was a group of Christians who had "gathered together and were praying" (Acts 12:5-12).

An Outreach Weekend was sponsored on the campus of the University of Wyoming by both Zion Church in Laramie and the campus church, St. Andrews. I arrived on Friday afternoon in order to participate in the evening of preparation and the early morning prayer service on Saturday. At 7:00 a.m. a small group of us assembled in the campus chapel. The lay leader made a few brief introductory comments, most of us knelt at our pews, and then different individuals began to lead in prayer. The prayers were short. After each prayer there was a brief pause, and someone else would pray. After 15 minutes of this my knees ached, and I thought we had prayed for everything that was going to happen over the weekend and for everyone who was going to be involved.

But people kept praying for the same people over and over again. I slid back in the seat with my head bowed to ease my aching knees and noticed that many of the group were sitting in their pews instead of kneeling. But the praying went on—and on—and on. We prayed for some of the same things over and over and kept adding new concerns. When the leader finally closed the prayer period, I looked at my watch. It was 8:00 a.m. It was my first experience in praying with a group for a full hour. Unless you have done it, you may wonder: How is it possible to find things to pray for during one solid hour? Is this "vain repetition," the making of many words?

While eating breakfast with some of the lay leaders of Zion, I discovered that there were many prayer groups in the Laramie church. All were the result of studying a method of prayer taught by Evelyn Christenson, known as the "Six S's." The first "S" is the principle "Subject by Subject," which means that one person leads in prayer on one subject while the rest pray silently on the same subject. They do not let their thoughts wander nor do they plan another subject for that time. In this way, there is complete concentration on one subject at a time both in silent prayer as well as the prayers spoken out loud. After that subject has been prayed about for a while, someone begins another subject and all pray with that subject in mind. Evelyn Christenson takes this concept of "Subject by Subject" from her interpretation of the phrase "with one accord" in Acts 1:14: "All these (the eleven apostles) with one accord devoted themselves to prayer, together with the women, Mary the mother of Jesus, and with His brothers." In her book she concludes: "When praying subject by subject, everyone is free to pray audibly in turn. But whether praying audibly or silently, all are praying in one accord on the same subject, not planning their own prayers in advance, and multiplying the power of all the prayers that are ascending simultaneously to God's throne."[9]

The promise of Jesus is "If two of you agree on earth about anything they ask, it will be done for them by My Father in heaven" (Matthew 18:19). The Greek word for

"agree together" is *sumphoneo,* the word from which our English word symphony comes. The prayers of Christians praying together is like the music of a beautiful symphony ascending to our Father, and He promises to do what those prayers ask.

In learning how to pray out loud, don't try to figure out what to say in an hour-long prayer meeting! If you are in such a meeting, listen to what others are praying, pray along with them in your thoughts, and then add simple, short prayers of your own out loud. This is an excellent way to learn how to pray, listening to others and beginning to verbalize additional prayers of your own.

Sometimes when a group prays together, either in a special prayer meeting, or to close another gathering such as a Bible study period, they may use a circle prayer. Either sitting or standing in a circle, sometimes holding hands, each one is expected to pray in turn around the circle. If you are in such a circle and don't know what to say, you can merely say, "Praise the Lord," or "Thank You, God," and, if you wish, mention one specific thing for which you want to thank God. It is also acceptable in most groups merely to say "pass" as a sign that you are not ready to pray right then, and the next person knows that he or she should continue the circle.

4. Ask in Many Ways and Places

A for Ask. Ask for your personal needs and the needs of others. Ask with others. And now think of where and how to ask.

Since prayer is talking to God as a Father, there can be no prescribed regulations as to where and how to do it. It can be done anywhere and in any way that communicates the message. All we can do here is describe ways and places that are found in Scripture or that Christians have found helpful. In our private lives, we can pray in devotions or our "quiet times" with the Lord, as well as in the needs of every moment of the day. With our family, we can pray at meal times, perhaps in our family devotions, and in special times of crisis or sickness.

Martin Luther suggested that when the child of God gets up in the morning, he should make "the sign of the holy cross" (make the outline of a cross on oneself) and say, "In the name of the Father and of the Son and of the Holy Ghost. Amen." Then, kneeling or standing, repeat the Creed, and the Lord's Prayer. Since most of the people in Luther's day were out of the habit of making their own prayers, he wrote this prayer which they could use.

I thank Thee, my heavenly Father, through Jesus Christ, Thy dear Son, that Thou hast kept me this night from all harm and danger; and I pray Thee that Thou wouldst keep me this day also from sin and every evil, that all my doings and life may please Thee. For into Thy hands I commend myself, my body and soul, and all things. Let Thy holy angel be with me, that the wicked foe may have no power over me. Amen.[10]

Luther suggested that when the Christian goes to bed at night, he also make the sign of the cross and say a similar prayer for the close of the day.

Some have found it helpful to be a part of a prayer group that meets weekly to share their concerns and pray for each other's needs and the needs of the church. Others find it helpful to have a "prayer partner," a person they can call anytime during the day, or meet with privately from time to time, to share concerns and pray together. Being part of a prayer chain is another way to get involved in praying for others. A telephone chain from one person to another sets up a system of sharing the needs of individuals or of the church and each person then praying for these needs.

In the year 466 A.D. there were earthquakes and calamities throughout Europe. In his concern the Bishop of Vienna decreed that the three days before the festival of the Ascension should serve as a period of prayer. Processions moved out of the churches into the fields so that Christians could pray for God's blessing on a good harvest right in the fields where they were planting their crops. This became an annual custom. It was so popular that by 591 A.D. it was prescribed for the entire church, and the Sunday before Ascension was listed on the church calendar as Rogate Sunday, or Prayer Sunday.

Not only do we go to church to pray or to the fields to pray for planting, but we pray in our homes, at our work, at our play, and in every place of life. We can remain in a constant attitude of prayer so that we do as Paul said, "Pray without ceasing" (1 Thessalonians 5:17). We also pray in many different ways and postures. Sometimes we pray with quiet thoughts in our minds. We may pray in an audible whisper. When we are in a group, we may pray loud and project our voice so that others can hear.

In the movie on personal witnessing, "Go and Tell," an African comes to the United States to learn about irrigation systems. The owner of an irrigation manufacturing system takes him to his hotel room where they visit for awhile. There the African asks if they might begin their work together with a prayer, and immediately drops to his knees to pray. The American, wanting to be friendly, kneels also while the African prays. Later, the American explains that he felt guilty. At first he did not know anything about his friend's religion. If he was a Muslim, he was facing toward Mecca—and if he was, then the American realized that he had the wrong end of himself facing that direction. But then he heard his friend pray "in the name of Christ," and a great burden fell from his shoulders.

Does it matter whether we kneel when we pray—or in what direction we face?

"You're not praying Scripturally," a man angrily protested to the leader of a seminar on prayer. When asked to explain, he said, "You're not holding up holy hands." He understood that this is the one position to be used at all times because it is mentioned by St. Paul in writing to Timothy: "I desire then that in every place the men should pray, lifting holy hands without anger or quarreling" (1 Timothy 2:8). See also Exodus 17:8-13; Psalm 63:3-4.[11]

But there are other examples of prayer posture in the Bible. Jesus in Gethsemane kneeled down and prayed (Luke

22:41). At the tomb of Lazarus, Jesus "lifted up His eyes" and talked to His Father (John 11:41). King Solomon in the Old Testament prostrated himself before the Lord when he prayed in the temple. David speaks about communing with God on his bed (Psalm 4:4). In our churches today some people kneel when they pray, others sit and bow their heads, while others stand. At one point in the history of the church it seems that standing was a sign of the resurrection. Tertullian, the early church father, went so far as to insist that "fasting and kneeling in worship on the Lord's Day is unlawful."[12] Saint Augustine makes the point that on Sundays "fasting is interrupted and we pray standing, because it is a sign of the resurrection."[13] Whatever the position or the place, the promise of God remains the same, "The eyes of the Lord are toward the righteous, and His ears toward their cry" (Psalm 34:15).

5. Let Us Pray

P is for Praise—Praise God for being God.

R is for Remember—Remember who you are.

A is for Ask—Ask what you want.

Let us continue to compose the prayers that we started in the previous two chapters. The prayers might go like this:

Prayer on Ministry

P for Praise:

Gracious Father, I praise You that You are the Lord of all institutions and that You love prisoners just as You love Charles and me.

R for Remember:

We are constantly tempted to sin, and I have done my share. I so often have judged the motives of those who are caught committing a crime, and I have wanted to see them pay for their wrong. Forgive my lack of compassion, my failure to help prevent crime, and my reluctance to visit those in prison.

A for Ask:

Help us to minister to them, to find ways to help

them understand and believe in your love and forgiveness through Christ. Show us how we can serve them so that they can find meaning and purpose in their lives in useful and constructive activities.

Prayer for a Sick Friend

P for Praise:

God, as a Father, You are concerned for Your children when they are sick. I thank and praise You for Your care and especially that You are a God who gives strength and comfort; and You heal when it is in Your will.

R for Remember:

We are so human and mortal that we need Your daily care and the strength You give. So often, Father, I fail to look to You for health, and I trust only the doctor for healing. Forgive me for my worrying and lack of faith.

A for Ask:

Please be with _____ , my friend, and by Your power and according to Your will, heal and restore him. Above all, give him faith to trust in Your love and in Your presence every moment. Help him commit himself to Your care both for this life and for eternal life with You forever.

Now Learn to Pray by Praying: _____

The Occasion: _____

The Theme: _____

P for Praise: _____

R for Remember: _____

A for Ask: _____

Y for Yield: _____

(Yield will be discussed in the next chapter.)

Bible Study and Action

1. From the following Bible passages, make a list of things for which to pray:

   1 Samuel 12:23 _____

   Psalm 50:15 _____

   Acts 4:23-31 _____

   Ephesians 3:14-19 _____

   Ephesians 6:18 _____

   James 5:14-16 _____

   1 Timothy 2:1-2 _____

   1 Timothy 4:5 _____

2. Make a prayer list, either in a special book or on file cards. Put one item on each line or card and list the date when you start praying for that person or item. Record the answers you see.

3. Agree with one or more persons to be prayer partners. Call each other at specific times when you agree to pray for special needs. You may also want to pray together over the telephone.

4. List from the following passages the places *where* the early Christians prayed:

   Acts 1:13-14 _____

   Acts 4:24, 31 _____

   Acts 9:11 _____

   Acts 10:9 _____

Acts 12: 5, 12 _____

Acts 16:25-26 _____

Acts 20:36 _____

Acts 21:5 _____

5. List 3 of the boldest things you ever asked for: How did God answer your prayers?

   a. _____

   b. _____

   c. _____

Chapter 5
Y for Yield

I was in my fourth year of college work at Concordia Seminary in St. Louis, working toward the B.A. degree that would be awarded at the end of the academic year. I hoped then to continue right into the seminary program, and in three years to have my childhood dream fulfilled—to become a pastor in the Lutheran Church.

But I was not satisfied. Most young men my age were in the military service, for it was a time of war (World War II). Theological students were going to school the year-round, since they were exempt from the draft. I was weary of studying and I wanted to get married. But most of all for the first time in my life I was not sure if I wanted to be a pastor! Ever since I was a little boy, folks asked me, "What are you going to be when you grow up?" I had always said, "I'm going to be a minister!"

So I began to search. I counseled with the Dean, took aptitude and interest tests, and read about other possible vocations. Still no satisfaction. Finally I quit the seminary and entered the U.S. Marine Corps. For the time being, I forgot my search and lived each day for itself without any concern for the future.

But I confronted my search again while on occupational duty in China. During my expriences in the Marine Corps, I saw life in its roughest and rawest form. I was drivien to the conclusion that there must be more to life than this! How could I be a part of something better? During the years of my search I had been asking the wrong question, "What do *I want* to do?" Now I finally reached the point where on my knees I submitted to God and asked, "God, what do *You want* me to do with my life?"

Having finally yielded, a peace soon came and with it the conviction that God's will for my life was that I should be a pastor. Ever since then this has been the key to my life, one to which I always return when I stray. "You are my Lord! Show me what You want me to do and I will do it." With that prayer of submission, peace always comes.

In prayer, "yield" is also the key word that brings it all together. It is the last line of our verse on learning how to pray:

Praise God for being God.
Remember who you are.
Ask what you want.
Yield to His will.

As we discuss "yielding to His will" in this chapter, we will need to devote some attention to the relationship of my will to God's will. This discussion is not directly connected to learning how to pray out loud, but it is necessary if we are to have the correct framework from which to compare the prayers which we do pray out loud. All of our prayers, both those in our private thoughts as well as those which we speak in public, are reflections of our basic understandings and beliefs. It is in the proper attitude of "yielding" that we can confidently and boldly pray.

1. I Pray in a Yielding Attitude

A child comes with bold confidence to his father with his needs and problems. It is true that some children cannot do this, but that is because the child-father relationship has been abused and damaged. In the ideal child-father relationship, the child knows that his father loves him and wants to give him what he asks. He also knows that his father makes the final decision as to whether he should or will give it to him. So he comes with a "yielding" attitude. This does not mean coming in such meekness that is one afraid to speak loudly his own will and desires. The child says, "I want a pair of roller skates," not, "if it is your will let me have a pair of roller skates."

a. Tell God What You Want

In the last chapter we said that prayer is asking, asking

God for specific needs and telling God our real desires. "Ask what you want," our prayer verse puts it. The asking is a bold presentation to God of the deep desires of our own will. Our Lord Jesus Christ Himself did that very thing when He prayed in the Garden of Gethsemane. There He exemplifies a man striving with God and presenting to God what he wants. Yet it is in an attitude of yielding to God's will. Jesus' example is not one of "stoic resignation to the inescapable, but a profound acceptance of the 'ways of God that are not the ways of men.' "[1] He did not meekly submit, but He pleaded to escape the punishment of hell. Examine carefully the accounts in Matthew and Luke. The first concern of Jesus' prayer is "Let this cup pass from Me" (Matthew 26:39) or "Remove this cup from Me" (Luke 22:42) and only then did He say, "Nevertheless not My will but Thine be done." He surrendered to the will of His Father only after seeking to change that will.

The concept of yielding to the will of God does not merely mean submission to whatever fate has determined for us. There is a time and a place for telling God what I want, for wrestling with God, for striving to compare my will with God's will, for even seeking to change God's attitude and plan. Martin Luther is a classic example (or some might consider him an extreme example) of striving with God in prayer. When he prayed for the healing of his beloved friend and co-worker, Melanchthon, he wrote, "This time I besought the Almighty with great vigor, I attacked Him with His own weapons, quoting from Scripture all the promises I could remember, that prayers should be granted, and said that He must grant my prayer, if I was henceforth to put faith in His promises."[2] Luther spoke often and passionately about trusting the promises of God, and when he came to the promises of the Scripture concerning prayer, he took them literally and demanded of God that He keep those promises. How can we learn to pray that boldly and actually demand of God that He answer our prayers? It begins, of course, with trust in the promises of God—when God says in Scripture, "Ask whatever you will, and it shall be done for you" (John 15:7), believe it. But we must go beyond those Scripture promises and add to them the word of Scripture which speaks about praying "according to the will of God" and those which speak about praying "in the Spirit."

b. Pray According to God's Will

The apostle John wrote his first epistle to those who "believe in the name of the Son of God that they might have eternal life" (1 John 5:13). Believers who are in that relationship with their Father in heaven can know, John adds, that "this is the confidence which we have in Him, that if we ask anything *according to His will* He hears us" (1 John 5:14). When we know that He hears us, there is no question but that we are sure that "we have obtained the requests made of Him" (1 John 5:15).

But how do we pray "according to God's will" so as to be sure that He hears us? It is essential, of course, that we desire to know the will of God. In some things we know very clearly what the will of God is in a general way as it applies to all people. But we are in hazy territory when, in the same things, we seek to know the will of God for a specific individual or situation. For instance, we know that it is the will of God that no person perish, but that all come to repentance and be saved (2 Peter 3:9). We can confidently pray "Lord, bring my son, Jim, to faith in Jesus"; "Lord, touch the heart of my neighbor, George, and lead him to faith." The problem comes when we get into the area of "when" and "how" that will of God should be implemented for Jim or George and even whether it will finally be accomplished. God restricts His sovereignty, as it were, and operates within the framework of human will. My son or my neighbor can always resist the work of the Spirit when He works in their hearts to bring them to faith. Even though it is God's will that they come to faith, and I pray that His will be done, they may never come to faith because of their own resistance.

We know that God's will for our individual lives is that

we be, as Paul says, "holy and free from immorality" (1 Thessalonians 4:3), and we can pray for that, without saying, "if it be Your will." But when it comes to praying for specific ways to be holy in our relationship to an employer at the time of a strike, we need to search for God's will and relate it to our own will. There is no easy answer, but as we seek to pray according to God's will, we remain in a posture of yielding, telling God what our own will is, and opening ourselves to His Spirit for direction and guidance.

c. Pray in the Spirit

The New Testament emphasizes our dependence on the Holy Spirit in our prayer life. Several times it uses, without explanation or detailed comment, the simple expression "pray in the Holy Spirit" (Jude 20), "pray at all times in the Spirit" (Ephesians 6:18). Romans 8:26-27 is the only place where the New Testament goes into detail as to how the Spirit is involved in our praying. There St. Paul explains that in our finite weakness we do not really know how to pray as we ought. Of course we don't—if we are to pray according to the will of God! So St. Paul assures us that "the Spirit Himself intercedes for us with sighs too deep for words" (v. 26). Then he explains further that the Spirit knows the mind of God, for He Himself is God as part of the Trinity; and He knows the mind and hearts of men. In this knowledge of the will of both God and man the Spirit "intercedes for the saints according to the will of God" (v. 27).

We pray "according to the will of God" by praying "in the Spirit." We present to God our requests, our needs, our will as we understand it in the attitude of yielding to the will of God, knowing that the Spirit will take these requests and strivings and wrestlings of ours and turn them into requests that fit into the will of God.

But there is even more good news about how God helps us pray, also when we pray out loud in public. In the opening versicle of the order of Matins, the pastor prays "O Lord, open Thou my lips," and the congregation responds, "And my mouth shall show forth Thy praise." That versicle and response is a direct quotation of Psalm 51:15. Today's English Version paraphrases that verse in these striking words: "Help me to speak, Lord, and I will praise You." Not only does God's Spirit turn our requests into the will of God, but here is a promise that God Himself will give us the words to say. When we pray out loud in public, we focus our thoughts on God our Father, and we trust Him to guide our thoughts and give us words to say.

d. Pray for the Glory of God

Another way of seeking to pray "according to the will of God" is to pray that all things be done to the glory of God. That is our overriding goal, that His name be glorified among men. In the Lord's Prayer we pray, "Hallowed by Thy name, Thy kingdom come" and that is why we want His will to be done on earth, because when that will is done then His kingdom does come, and His name is hallowed: His name is honored and held sacred. Bloesch says that the "overriding motivation" of the Christian in his prayer life is to "glorify God and to discover His will for our lives."[3]

But what is it that will glorify the name of God? That's the big question! That is where the struggle takes place between what we want and ask and what is God's will. Martin Luther again is a dramatic example of how bold one can become in his prayers when he is praying that God's name be glorified.

In 1540 Luther's good friend, Frederick Myconius, became deathly sick. He himself expected that he would die within a short time, as did most of his close associates. He wrote to Luther with trembling hand to give him fond farewell, for he loved Luther much. When Luther received the letter, he immediately sent back a reply which read: "I command thee in the name of God to live because I still have need of thee in the work of reforming the church." Later in the letter he explained, "The Lord will never let me hear that thou art dead, but will permit thee to survive me. For this I am praying, this is my will, and may *my will be done*, because *I seek only to glorify the name of God*."[4] When Luther's letter

arrived, Myconius had already lost the ability to speak, but in a short time he recovered and, true enough, he did survive Luther by two months.

In commenting upon this example of Luther, Hallesby says that we are bold in prayer when we can look into the eye of God and say to Him, "Thou knowest that I am not praying for personal advantage, nor to avoid hardship, not that my own will in any way should be done, but only for this that Thy name might be glorified."[5]

To summarize this section on praying with a yielding attitude, I tell God my will and seek to determine whether there is any way possible that my will can be done in such a way that God is glorified. As I do this, I pray "in the Spirit" seeking to pray "according to the will of God." In practice this means that I don't meekly pray, "Lord, if it can somehow be in Your will, lead me to a job as a computer technician, and let me earn enough for a good living for my family." Rather I boldly confront God and say, "You have promised that You will give whatever I ask. You have given me the talents to be a computer technician, and now I ask you to give me a job in which I can use those skills in a way in which I can support my family and bring glory to Your name." If it is God's will to lead me into a different kind of work, He will show me, but I start by telling Him what I want. Luther said that the most powerful prayer is prayer with "sobs and tears" as I lay before Him my will and claim His promises to hear me, and I can do that in "a yielding attitude."[6]

2. Yield to God's Answers

Y for Yield. Yield to His will.

We present our will to God as we tell Him our needs and wants and desires in a spirit of seeking to glorify His name, then having His will done in and through us and expecting answers to those prayers. In that expectancy the key word again is "yield." We yield to whatever answer God determines.

a. Look for Answers

We expect answers to our prayers because we really

believe that God hears and answers. It would not be worth asking if we did not expect an answer. But we need to remain open to whatever the answer might be, no matter how bold or demanding we have been in praying. It is interesting to read how Martin Luther, despite the extreme examples quoted above in which he demanded of God that His will be done in the healing of Myconius and of Melanchthon, could still speak of answers in terms of God's will. He said, "It is not a bad but a very good thing if the opposite of what we pray for appears to happen. Just as it is not a good sign if our prayers eventuate in the fulfillment of all we ask for."[7]

In that spirit, then, ready to yield to God's answers, we do not slip into the habit of prescribing to God what the answers should be. We learn to pray in the form of requests. We tell God our desires, but we do not dictate the answers. We leave the final decision to His wisdom and will.

b. Believe That God Changes

"If everything is done according to God's will, if He makes every decision, then why pray?" Satan plagues many Christians with that thought. But as with most tactics the devil uses, it is a tricky half truth. God's nature and essence does not change. God says, "I the Lord do not change" (Malachi 3:6). Of Jesus, the Son of God, Scripture says, "Jesus Christ is the same yesterday and today and forever" (Hebrews 13:8). God's ultimate will and purpose does not change. On the other hand, Scripture teaches that prayer does effect a change in God, at least in the way that God accomplishes His will and plan. We need to find a way to harmonize those two statements that God does not change and that prayer does change Him.

Look first at some examples given in Scripture of the results of prayer. When God saw His chosen people worshiping the golden calf, He said to His faithful servant, Moses, "Let Me alone, that My wrath may burn hot against them and I may consume them; but of you I will make a great nation" (Exodus 32:10). But Moses would not leave God alone. He prayed, he pleaded, he admonished, and "the Lord repented of the evil which He thought to do to His people" (Exodus 32:14). God revealed to Amos His plan of judgment against His people, a judgment first of locusts and then of fire. In each instance, Amos prayed, and the record says, "The Lord repented," that is, He changed His mind and He said, "it shall not be" (Amos 7:1-6).

How do we harmonize the statements that God does not change with the fact that the prayers of human beings are said to lead Him to "repent" or change? Bloesch suggests that we think of God's ultimate will as inflexible. He does not change in what He wants to accomplish. But the ways in which He implements that will are flexible. "He does not change His final purpose, but He does alter His methods for realizing that purpose."[8] Some people find it helpful to think of the "permissive" will of God in which He allows us the freedom to operate according to our own will even though all things are still under His providential control.

In summary, then, we pray in a spirit that yields to the will of God according to the measure of our faith, and we are ready to yield to the answers which He gives. But we do look for answers and expect them according to the things for which we have prayed. We believe that our prayers do have an effect and that God can change in response to those prayers.

c. Wrestle with God in Prayer

Scripture tells us how Jacob in a physical way wrestled with God in the form of a man through the night. In the morning when God blessed Jacob, He changed his name to "Israel," which means, "He who strives with God," for God said, "you have striven with God and with men and have prevailed" (Genesis 32:24-30). In the ministry of Jesus a Canaanite woman begged for help for her demon possessed daughter, but Jesus rebuffed her saying that He was sent only to the lost sheep of the house of Israel. She refused to be put off and pleaded for a few crumbs. Jesus answered her prayer, and her daughter was healed (Matthew 15:21-28).

We too wrestle and strive with God in prayer. We do so

in order to discover the full scope of His will. We struggle to overcome our own will and bring it into harmony with His will so that He may be glorified. This does at times involve questioning God's will, as Jesus did in Gethsemane, but always in the spirit of submission to His final decision. There are times when there are several ways in which God's will can be accomplished and through our wrestling with God we seek to discover the best way to do it.

d. Accept God's Answer

But the spirit behind all our striving is our attitude of yielding to God's answers. So whenever the answer comes, we accept it. The answer, however, may not come for a while, but we remember that "delays are not denials." And as we wait for God's answer to come, we don't make our own answers. Lois Johnson tells of a woman who prayed, "Lord, give my daughter a good husband," and then systematically introduced her to every eligible man in the country.[9] It is true that sometimes God answers our prayers through the action that He expects of us, but then He shows us the direction and course of that action.

Sometimes, however, God's answer is "no." As children who trust the Father's wisdom and love, we accept that answer.

Sometimes the answer which God gives is different than the one for which we prayed, and it is not really a "no" after all. When Paul begged God to remove his "thorn" in the flesh, God responded, not by removing the "thorn," but by giving Paul the strength to bear it. He used it as a means to keep Paul humble and to train him to trust in Him rather than in his own strength (2 Corinthians 12:7-10).

But if we continue to pray for a specific need and see no response from God whatever, this might be cause to evaluate our prayer. There are prayers which we cannot expect God to answer. The problem may be in us rather than in God. Murphey lists five kinds of prayers which are not answered:

(1) *Destructive prayers,* like those some people prayed

during the 1979—81 hostage crisis, "God, kill those Iranians."

(2) *Self-centered, me-only, prayers,* like those of the small child who wants what he wants regardless of the inconvenience or hardship his prayers may cause for others.

(3) *Unmeant prayers,* prayers that are mouthed because others expect them of us, or when we join others in a hymn or liturgy and say without meaning it, "take my silver and my gold, not a mite would I withhold."

(4) *Unwise prayers,* asking for a job with adventure even when we know it means danger and temptation. It would also be like the student who didn't know how to answer the question on his examination, "What is the capital of Illinois?" So he wrote "Boston" and then prayed, "Lord, make Boston the capital of Illinois."

(5) *Prayers for an easy time,* asking for a job where we can loaf half the time, or for an inheritance so we don't have to work. God never promised an easy life.[10]

Lois Johnson says that when she does not see any answers to her prayers, she asks herself such questions as: Do I have any unforgiven sin blocking the answer? Do I understand the ways in which the answers come? Am I praying in line with God's will? Am I praying in faith?[11]

One area of prayer that causes serious problems for some Christians is that of healing. If I pray for healing and it does not come, I am tempted to think that it was because I did not have enough faith. But that attitude makes faith the agent of healing rather than God. Prayer is asking Almighty God for healing. As Christians we submit to Him as a Father who loves us His children and cares for us. Healing is God's response, and He will not be controlled by any prescriptions that we give Him. He heals one but lets another suffer. For the healing, we praise him. For the suffering, we trust His compassion in the moment of pain. "Faith is to believe that He cares and He can and does intervene at unexpected places in unexpected ways, but it is not for us to define those places and ways. Only God can decide those things."[12]

Even suffering can be God's will for us as it was for St.

Paul with his thorn in the flesh. St. Peter puts it very clearly when he says, "So then those who *suffer* **according to God's will** should submit themselves to their faithful Creator and continue to do good" (1 Peter 4:19 NIV).

Y for Yield. Yield to the will of God! That is what we are to do when we accept God's answers to our prayers, whether that will be healing or suffering—we give God all glory and praise.

e. Close Your Prayer

When Jesus gave His disciples the model prayer which we know as the Lord's Prayer, He said, "when you pray, pray like this," but He did not put an ending or conclusion on that prayer. It ended with "Deliver us from evil" (Matthew 6:13). The early Christians evidently felt an immediate need to add some kind of conclusion which expressed confidence in God's promise to hear prayer and faith in His power to answer. So some early manuscripts include the words: "For thine is the kingdom and the power and the glory, forever. Amen."

In either case, whether these words were in the prayer as Jesus taught it or were added by some obscure early disciple of Jesus, they are a fitting close to the prayer, for they express faith in the God to whom the prayer is addressed and give glory to Him. The same thoughts could be expressed in different ways. The briefest summary of a close which expresses confidence that God has heard and will answer our prayer is the single word, "Amen," which means, "Yes, I believe it will be so."

But Christians have developed the custom to add, before saying that final "amen," other phrases to conclude their prayers, phrases which express their faith in privilege and right, that they have to come to the Father because Jesus Christ has forgiven them their sins and brought them into God's family. So they add, "In Jesus' name," or some variation as "through Jesus Christ, Thy Son, our Lord"; "I pray this Father, in the name of Your Son"; "for Jesus' sake"; "I pray to You in the blessed name of Jesus, my Savior." (See

Chapter 3 for a discussion of the phrase "in the name of Jesus.")

3. Yield to Growth in Prayer

There is only one way to learn how to swim—moving your arms and legs in the water. You can read all the books which explain the theory and listen to an instructor explain exactly what to do, but you can't learn how to swim until you get in the water and try it. But after you have taken your first desperate strokes, you need to practice. You swim and swim and swim in order to learn how to swim better, and to do it with more ease than struggle.

It is the same with prayer. You can read this book and hear lectures on how to pray in public or in private, but you will not really learn how to pray until you begin to do it—follow this with practice and practice and practice. That involves a "yielding" too, in the sense of yielding to a commitment to do it. When there are opportunities to pray in public, take them. But those opportunities may be few. Yet you can still practice, practice in your private meditations, in your family devotions, with your spouse, or with a prayer partner.

As you form your prayers with the key words: Praise, Remember, Ask, Yield, these words will become more meaningful, and you can become freer to expand the content of your prayers. But there are other areas of growth, such as growth in honest conversation, in being specific, and in constant prayer.

a. Growth in Honest Conversation

"God, I don't feel like praying right now. My heart feels empty but I know that You understand, so I'll just talk to You...." That was one person's response to reading a prayer from a prayer book which used high sounding phrases which the reader could not make his own. So, he just told God how he felt and talked to Him. That is prayer, prayer in honest conversation.

In talking to God as our Father, we can share with Him

our dry periods, our valleys and plateaus, as well as our mountain tops, and as we talk honestly with God, we can learn to be more honest with ourselves and admit our weaknesses and our needs.

This kind of honest conversation must be in words rather than in vague thoughts. We can practice formulating those words by speaking them in our thoughts or saying them quietly aloud even in private. Then when we are to pray in public, our conversation will flow much easier, for we will be doing in public only what we have been practicing in private.

b. Growth in Being Specific

As a father passed the bedroom of his little daughter one night, he heard her saying the alphabet out loud. He stopped to ask what she was doing. "I'm saying my prayers," she said. When the father wanted to know how reciting the alphabet could be saying prayers, she explained, "I can't think of the right words to pray tonight, so I'm saying all the letters. God knows what I'm thinking, so He'll put them together for me."[13]

God does indeed know what we think, and He promises that even before we ask He will answer. Yet he invites and commands us to pray because He wants us to talk to Him. He wants us to put into words the thoughts and desires of our hearts. It is an expression of our relationship to Him, and the more we talk to Him, the easier it is to become specific. In guidelines prepared for composing general prayers for use in a congregational worship service, Jaroslav Vajda speaks pointedly of being specific when praying. He says that while the prayer must be general enough to fit most worshipers, it must also be "specific enough to deal with real concerns." In more detail, he suggests that the word "bless" should not appear more than once. Instead the request should specify what kind of blessing is being sought, such as "arm with courage," "endow with patience," "fill with wisdom." That is good advice also for private prayer. So when I pray for a child or friend, or when I open a meeting with prayer, or pray before a meal, for example, which of the following prayers is more specific?

"We thank You, Father, for this meal and our fellowship at this table. Bless us all for Jesus' sake."

OR

"Father, You are good to us in providing us this food and the opportunity to be together. We thank You for both, and pray that You would help us receive this food in gratitude. Please use this food to strengthen our bodies, and make our conversation enjoyable so we may be enriched to serve You, for Jesus' sake."

c. Growth in Constant Prayer

Perhaps what is most helpful in learning how to pray in public is practice in talking to God repeatedly throughout the day. "Practice the presence of God," being conscious that He is with us constantly and is available so we can speak to Him in our thoughts no matter what else we are doing.

During a meeting of several days' duration at a motel, I met my friend, Elmer, at six o'clock one morning to go out to jog. We had met like this before, but this particular morning Elmer said, "I can't talk much today, I've got a lot of praying to do." And he did. That was his way of getting 20 minutes each morning to talk to God about the concerns of that day, to pray as he jogged.

That takes practice, a determined effort to be conscious of God's presence and to develop the habit of talking to Him. Martin Luther was convinced that every Christian can find a way to do this. He said:

"There is no Christian who does not have time to pray without ceasing. . . . no one is so heavily burdened with his labor, but that if he will, he can, while working, speak with God in his heart, lay before Him his need and that of other men, ask for help, make petition, and in all this exercise and strengthen his faith."[14]

(See Section 4 of Chapter 1 for further discussion of the topic "Be Conscious of the Presence of God.")

4. Let Us Pray

Now let us finish composing the prayers that we started in the previous chapters:

Prayer on Ministry

P for Praise: Praise God for being God.

Gracious Father, I praise You that You are the Lord of all institutions and that You love prisoners just as You love Charles and me.

R for Remember: Remember who you are.

We are constantly tempted to sin, and I have done my share. I so often have judged the motives of those who are caught committing a crime, and I have wanted to see them pay for their wrong. Forgive my lack of compassion, my failure to help prevent crime, and my reluctance to visit those in prison.

A for Ask: Ask what you want.

Help us to minister to them, to find ways to help them understand and believe in Your love and forgiveness through Christ. Show us how we can serve them so that they can find meaning and purpose in their lives in useful and constructive activities.

Y for Yield: Yield to His will.

Fill us with Your Spirit and show us Your will, for we seek to bring honor and glory to Your name in all that we do, for we do it in the name of our Lord and Savior Jesus Christ.

Prayer for a Sick Friend

P for Praise: Praise God for being God.

God, as a Father, You are concerned for Your children when they are sick. I thank and praise You for Your care and especially that You are a God who gives strength and comfort. I know that You can heal when it is Your will.

R for Remember: Remember who you are.

We are so human and mortal that we need the daily care and strength that You give. So often, Father, we fail to look to You for health and we trust only the doctor for healing. Forgive us for our worrying and lack of faith.

A for Ask: Ask what you want.

Please be with _____ _____ , my friend, and by Your power and according to Your will heal and restore him. Above all give him faith to trust in Your love and in Your presence every moment. Help him commit himself to Your care both for this life and for eternal life with You forever.

Y for Yield: Yield to His will.

Gracious Father, You have promised to hear Your children who call upon You. I believe You will hear me now and answer according to Your promise, and in Your wisdom. Let Your will be done and give me as one of Your children the faith to accept it through Jesus our Savior. Amen.

As you now come to the close of this book on learning how to pray in public, I hope that you have taken your first strokes, like a swimmer learning how to swim, and that you will continue to grow by studying and by praying. Set aside a daily "quiet time." Be active in a group that studies the Scriptures and prays together. As you continue to use the acrostic: P for Praise, R for Remember, A for Ask, and Y for Yield, these four actions will become so much a part of your thoughts that you won't even think about the words which describe them. You will automatically do them.

That is my prayer for you.

Bible Study and Action

1. "Learn of Jesus Christ to pray" the hymn writer says. Examine the practice of prayer in the life of Jesus by filling in the blanks. What did you learn from doing this?

   Luke 4:42 _____

   Luke 5:16 _____

   Luke 6:12 _____

Luke 9:18 _____

Luke 9:28-29 _____

2. Luther explained that he would take a verse of Scripture and find four strands which could be woven together from that passage. Take one of your favorite Bible verses and try it (or use Matthew 28:16-20):

Instruction _____

Thanks _____

Confession _____

Petition and Intercession _____

3. Jesus Christ, who sits in power at the right hand of God, prays for us. According to the following passages, what is the main concern of Jesus' prayer? How is that different from the Holy Spirit praying for us?

1 John 2:1 _____

Romans 8:34 _____

Compare Romans 8:26-27 _____

4. Read about the healing of Hezekiah in 2 Kings 20:1-7. When the prophet Isaiah delivered the message that Hezekiah should get his house in order, since God had decided that he should die in his illness and not get well, should he have prayed, "Let Your will, O God, be done," and submitted to death? What did he pray? Did God change His mind?

5. Turn back to the prayers at the end of Chatper 4, and now write the last paragraph adding the Y for Yield.

6. Write some prayers using the outline.
   Praise
   Remember
   Ask
   Yield

Footnotes for Chapter 1

[1] Maxie Dunnam, *The Workbook of Living Prayer* (Nashville: The Upper Room, 1974), p. 7.

[2] Ibid., p. 15.

[3] Lois Johnson, *Either Way, I Win, A Guide for Growth in the Power of Prayer* (Minneapolis: Augsburg Publishing House, 1979), p. 27.

[4] Ole Christian Hallesby, *Prayer*, trans. Clarence J. Carlsen, 1931 (Minneapolis: Augsburg Publishing House, 1975), p. 17.

[5] Ibid., p. 16.

[6] Ray C. Stedman, *Jesus Teaches on Prayer* (Waco: Word Books, 1975), p. 7.

[7] Nicolas Herman (Brother Lawrence), *The Practice of the Presence of God* (New York: Fleming H. Revell, 1895), p. 8. As quoted by Cecil Murphey, *Prayerobics* (Waco: Word Books, 1979), p. 22.

[8] Oscar E. Feucht, *The Practice of Prayer* (St. Louis: Concordia Publishing House, 1956), p. 6.

[9] Hallesby, p. 135.

Footnotes for Chapter 2

[1] Charlie W. Shedd, *How to Develop a Praying Church* (Nashville: Abingdon Press, 1964).

[2] Ardis Whitman, "Six Special Powers of Prayer," *Reader's Digest* (April 1980), p. 94.

[3] Hallesby p. 140.

[4] Whitman, p. 94.

[5] Colin Brown, ed., *The New International Dictionary of New Testament Theology I* (Grand Rapids: Zondervan, 1977), p. 99.

[6] Charles Colson, *Life Sentence* (Waco: Word Books, 1979), pp. 105—06.

[7] Martin Luther, *What Luther Says, An Anthology*, compiled by Ewald M. Plass (St. Louis: Concordia Publishing House, 1959), Vol. II, p. 1,082.

Footnotes for Chapter 3

[1] Kieth Gerberding, *That We May Grow . . . in Prayer* (St. Louis: The Board for Evangelism, n.d.), p. 5.

[2] Maxie Dunnam, p. 31.

[3] Donald G. Bloesch, *The Struggle of Prayer* (San Francisco: Harper & Row Publishers, 1980), p. 47.

[4] Dunnam, p. 73.

[5] *A Short Explanation of Dr. Martin Luther's Small Catechism* (St. Louis: Concordia Publishing House, 1943), p. 143.

[6] Lois Walfrid Johnson, p. 115.

[7] Evelyn Christenson and Viola Blake, *What Happens When Women Pray* (Wheaton, IL: Victor Books, 1975), pp. 24-25.

Footnotes for Chapter 4

[1] Hallesby, p. 16.

[2] Erwin Kurth, *Catechetical Helps* (Brooklyn: The Studio Press, 1935), p. 118.

[3] *Small Catechism*, p. 146.

[4] Stedman, p. 131.

[5] Edmund McKendree Bounds, *Preacher and Prayer*, Tract by the Department of Evangelism, (Wilmore, Ky.: Ashbury Theological Seminary, 1974), p. 29.

[6] Charlie W. Shedd, *How to Develop a Praying Church* (Nashville: Abingdon Press, 1964).

[7] Karen Merkel, "How to Pray for Your Missionary" (Minneapolis: World Mission Prayer League, n.d.).

[8] Cecil Murphey, *Prayerobics*, Getting Started and Staying Going (Waco: Word Books, 1979), p. 95.

[9] Evelyn Christenson, p. 41. The "S's" in the "Six S's" method are: (1) Subject by subject; (2) Short prayers; (3) Simple prayers; (4) Specific prayer requests; (5) Silent periods; and (6) Small groups.

[10] *Small Catechism*, p. 22.

[11] Christenson, p. 83.

[12] Saint Augustine, *De Corona* 3, 4, as quoted in the *Concordia Journal*, "Along the Horizons," Martin H. Scharlemann (May 1980), p. 91.

[13] Saint Augustine, *Epistola* 55, as quoted in the *Concordia Journal*, "Along the Horizons," Martin H. Scharlemann (May 1980), p. 91.

Footnotes for Chapter 5

[1] Donald G. Bloesch, p. 77.

[2] Gengt R. Hoffman, *Luther and the Mystics* (Minneapolis: Augsburg Publishing House, 1976), p. 196.

[3] Bloesch, p. 71.

[4] Hallesby, pp. 130 f.

[5] Ibid, p. 131.

[6] Martin Luther, *Luther's Works*, American Edition, Vol. 7, ed. J. Pelikan (St. Louis: Concordia Publishing House, 1965), p. 375.

[7] *Martin Luther: Lectures on Romans*, Library of Christian Classics, edited and translated by Wilhelm Pauck, (Philadelphia: Westminster Press, 1961), Vol. XV, p. 240.

[8] Bloesch, p. 74.

[9] Johnson, p. 58.

[10] Murphey, pp. 125—29.

[11] Johnson, pp. 116 f.

[12] Hubert Beck, *What Should I Believe* (St. Louis: Concordia Publishing House, 1980), p. 41.

[13] Kent R. Hunter, *New Life in Jesus Christ* (Detroit: Church Growth Analysis and Learning Center, 1980), p. 15.

[14] Hugh Thompson Kerr Jr., ed. *A Compend of Luther's Theology* (Philadelphia: Westminster Press, 1943), p. 109.

Bibliography

Barclay, William. *A Guide to Daily Prayer.* New York: Harper & Row, 1962.
A book of prayers in contemporary language for all occasions, with a helpful introduction on prayers.

Bloesch, Donald G. *The Struggle of Prayer.* San Francisco: Harper & Row, Publishers, 1980.
A theology of prayer which sees prayer as dialog with a living God, more than as recitation and meditation.

Christenson, Evelyn, and Viola Blake. *What Happens When Women Pray.* Wheaton, IL: Victor Books, 1975.
Simple explanations and directions to help people (not just women) learn how to pray. The materials have been used in hundreds of prayer seminars.

Dunnam, Maxie. *The Workbook of Living Prayer.* Nashville: The Upper Room, 1974.
With practical exercises this book seeks to help people develop a meaningful prayer life and learn to pray for others.

Feucht, Oscar E. *The Practice of Prayer.* St. Louis: Concordia Publishing House, 1956. (Out of print)
A helpful booklet which attempts to put the Biblical teaching about prayer in practice in the Christian's life.

Hallesby, Ole Christian. *Prayer.* Translated by Clarence J. Carlsen. Minneapolis: Augsburg Publishing House, 1931.
Considered a classic on prayer—to deepen and enrich prayer life.

Johnson, Lois Walfrid. *Either Way, I Win,* A Guide for Growth in the Power of Prayer. Minneapolis: Augsburg Publishing House, 1979.
The personal story of a woman who grew in prayer as she experienced cancer and its treatment.

Malz, Betty. *Prayers That Are Answered.* Lincoln, Virginia: Chosen Books, 1980.
The story of a woman who had "died," returned to life, and then began a remarkable series of adventures in prayer.

Murphey, Cecil. *Prayerobics,* A Guide for Developing Your Prayer Fitness. Waco: Word Books, 1979.
From his own personal experience, the author seeks to make prayer a constant part of one's daily activity.

Murphy, Miriam. *Prayer in Action,* A Growth Experience. Nashville: Abingdon, 1979.

Exploring Christian mystics as well as contemporary religious movements, this book seeks to help one grow in the healing of the whole person in prayer.

Shedd, Charlie W. *How to Develop a Praying Church.* Nashville: Abingdon Press, 1964.
The author tells of his own experience as a pastor in leading his congregation to pray for one another.

Shoemaker, Helen Smith. *Prayer and Evangelism.* Waco: Word Books, 1974.
Pray, talk, act is the author's three-step remedy for effective evangelism.

Stedman, Ray C. *Jesus Teaches on Prayer,* A Discovery Bible Study Book. Waco: Word Books, 1975.
The author guides the reader through the teachings of Jesus on prayer and seeks to give them a new sense of what our prayer life should be.